SEND ME?

THE ITINERANCY IN CRISIS

DONALD E.
MESSER
E D I T O R

ABINGDON PRESS/Nashville

SEND ME?

THE ITINERACY IN CRISIS

This book is printed on recycled, acid-free paper.

Library of Congress Cataloging-in-Publication Data

Send Me? : the itineracy in crisis / Donald E. Messer, editor.
p. cm.
Includes bibliographical references.
Contents: Itineracy in early Methodism / Russell E. Richey—When Korea abolished guaranteed appointments / Joon Kwan Un—Without reserve / William B. Oden—Spiritual discernment in consultation / M. Kent Millard—Reaffirming the covenant in itineracy / Donald H. Treese—Who is the client? the clergy or the congregation? / Lyle E. Schaller—A generic lay perspective / Sally B. Geis—Crossing cultural, racial, and gender boundaries / Susan M. Morrison and Gilbert H. Caldwell—Conflicting covenants / Bonnie J. Messer and Denise Johnson Stovall—Married to the church and to each other / Kenneth L. Waters and Lydia J. Waters—Liberation for a culture in crisis / Rebecca S. Chopp—Where do we go from here? / Donald E. Messer.

ISBN 0-687-36910-X (alk. paper)

1. Itinerancy (Church polity)—United Methodist Church (U.S.) 2. United Methodist Church (U.S.)—Clergy—Appointment, call, and election. 3. Methodist Church—Clergy—Appointment, call, and election. 4. Clergy—Relocation. I. Messer, Donald E.
BX8388.S37 1991
262′ . 1476—dc20 91-12719
CIP

MANUFACTURED IN THE UNITED STATES OF AMERICA

TO

Elaine and John Blinn
Grace and Gilbert Caldwell
Karla and Darrel Leach
Minnietta and M. Kent Millard
Paula and Paul Murphy
Sharilee and Bill Selby

AND TO

All the Wonderful Itinerant Pastors and Spouses
of the
South Dakota and Rocky Mountain Conferences

CONTENTS

ACKNOWLEDGMENTS

The contributors to this volume graciously accepted their assignments within the pressure of very short time frames. I commend to you their essays as excellent examples of reflective practical theology.

No book can be written or published without the assistance of countless persons. Any listing runs the risk of missing those who have contributed; yet failure to give acknowledgments would be unforgivable. I stand in debt to so many individuals who have contributed their services and insights to this manuscript.

Special words of appreciation are due my colleagues at The Iliff School of Theology, Sally B. Geis and A. James Armstrong. This book evolved from an essay we co-authored, which advocated the need for opening a dialogue on the future of the United Methodist itineracy. Later, Abingdon Press, through editor Paul Franklyn, invited me to develop this book. The strong support and assistance of my colleagues and Abingdon Press have been invaluable.

Virginia Dorjahn, Executive Secretary to the President of The Iliff School of Theology for the past thirty-five years, again provided her extraordinary professional care and competence to the tasks of manuscript preparation and correspondence. Special thanks are given for the extra efforts of Alberta Smith, who, with assistance from Margaret Manion and Lucile Schweppe, typed this manuscript.

Gratitude is also due my very special friends and colleagues who assisted in editing the final manuscript: John P. Blinn, Suzanne Calvin, David Dolsen, Thomas H. Matheney, Paul E. and Paula

Murphy, Sara J. Myers, Margaret H. Rush, Roy I. Sano, Jean Miller Schmidt, William P. Selby, Dwight and Sonia Strawn, J. Charles Schuster, O. Gerald and Rose Trigg, James P. and Rebecca Wenger-Monroe. With assistance from Paul A. Sears, Paul Millette, and the staff of the Ira J. Taylor Library at Iliff, they made it possible for this book to be completed on schedule. Invaluable consultative advice was provided by Laura Deming, James Kirby, Kathy Nickerson Sage, Phyllis Tyler-Wayman, and Edward Wimberly.

My books are never written without the involvement of my family. My wife, Bonnie, co-authored a chapter, and our two college-age children, Christine M. Messer and Kent D. Messer, provided indispensable research assistance. Without their sustaining love and encouragement, this ministry of writing would not be possible.

CONTRIBUTORS

Gilbert H. Caldwell is the West Chester District Superintendent of the Eastern Pennsylvania Conference. Former Associate General Secretary of the General Commission on Religion and Race, he has served United Methodist pastorates in Massachusetts, New York, Connecticut, and Pennsylvania. A leader in the civil rights movement, he is the author of *Race, Racism and Reconciliation.*

Rebecca S. Chopp is associate professor of systematic theology at the Candler School of Theology, Emory University. Previously, she was coordinator of ministry programs and assistant professor of theology at the University of Chicago Divinity School. A United Methodist pastor, she served in Kansas and Missouri. She has authored *Praxis of Suffering: An Interpretation of Liberation and Political Theologies* and *The Power to Speak: Feminism, Language, God.*

Sally B. Geis is director of the Iliff Institute for Lay and Clergy Education, The Iliff School of Theology. A sociologist, she has authored numerous scholarly articles and currently is clinical associate professor of psychiatry at the University of Colorado Health Sciences Center. A lay member of General and Jurisdictional Conferences, she serves on numerous United Methodist national and conference committees.

Joon Kwan Un is dean and professor of Christian education at the School of Theology, Yonsei University, Seoul, Korea. A Methodist clergyman, he has served as University Chaplain and senior pastor of Chung Dong First Methodist Church in Seoul. He has been an active leader of the Methodist Church in Korea. He is the author of *A Theology of Education* and *The Context of Christian Education.*

Bonnie J. Messer is a licensed psychologist engaged in private practice in Englewood, Colorado. An adjunct professor at the University of Denver, she previously served as associate director of the university's counseling center. A consultant to the Partners in Ministry program at The Iliff School of Theology, she has led workshops on clergy spouses, adult transitions, and couples communications. Her diagnostic instrument, "The Adult Self-Perception Profile," is used to assess self-esteem in adults.

Donald E. Messer is president of The Iliff School of Theology. Currently, he also serves as president of the Association of United Methodist Theological Schools. Previously he served in South Dakota as a pastor and president of Dakota Wesleyan University. He is the author of *Christian Ethics and Political Action* and *Contemporary Images of Christian Ministry* (selected by the Academy of Parish Clergy as one of the ten best books of 1989).

M. Kent Millard is senior pastor of First United Methodist Church, Sioux Falls, South Dakota. He has served other pastorates in South Dakota and Massachusetts, as well as being a district superintendent. Elected to General and Jurisdictional Conferences, he is active in the Lay Academy for Spiritual Formation. He has authored various articles and book chapters, and taught numerous workshops across the United States related to the parish ministry.

Susan M. Morrison is bishop of the Philadelphia Area. Prior to election to the episcopacy, she served as a pastor, district superintendent, conference council director, and short-term missionary to Brazil. She chairs the committee developing the new *Book of Worship.* Active in ecumenical relations, she has been a member of the World Methodist Council.

William B. Oden is bishop of the Louisiana Area. He has served as pastor at churches in Enid, Norman, and Oklahoma City, Oklahoma. He served as an adjunct faculty member for Phillips Graduate Seminary. He is the author of three books: *Wordeed: Evangelism in Biblical/Wesleyan Perspective, Liturgy as Life Journey,* and *Oklahoma Methodism in the Twentieth Century.*

Russell E. Richey is associate dean for academic programs and research professor of church history at Duke University Divinity School. A United Methodist pastor in the North Carolina Conference, he previously taught at Drew University. Author of numerous scholarly historical articles, he has co-edited three books: *American*

Civil Religion, Denominationalism, and *Re-thinking Methodist History.*

Lyle E. Schaller, an ordained member of the East Ohio Conference, serves as a consultant to the Yokefellow Institute in Richmond, Indiana, and the J. M. Ormond Center for Research and Development at Duke University Divinity School. Author of more than eight hundred articles and three dozen books, among the most recent books are *Choices for Churches, Create Your Own Future,* and *The Seven-Day-A-Week Church.* In 1989 Hartford Seminary named him the most influential leader among American Protestants.

Denise Johnson Stovall is associate editor of *The United Methodist Reporter* in Dallas, Texas. A recipient of the Stoody-West Fellowship, she has won journalism awards from the Associated Church Press and United Methodist Communications. A pastor's spouse, she serves on the national board of directors of SPICE (a support system for women and men whose spouses are clergy).

Donald H. Treese is associate general secretary of the Board of Higher Education and Ministry, Nashville, Tennessee. He has served pastorates in Carlisle and Altoona, Pennsylvania, and has been elected to numerous general and jurisdictional conferences. He was chairperson of the National Commission to Study the Itineracy in 1978–79, and the World Methodist Council on Theological Education. He has published numerous articles and book chapters.

Kenneth L. Waters is pastor of the Vermont Square United Methodist Church in Los Angeles, California. A Ph.D. candidate in New Testament at Fuller Theological Seminary, he serves as a "Growth Plus" consultant for the Board of Discipleship. He and his wife, Lydia, are contributing editors for *Clergy Couples Connect* and were featured as a clergy couple on the "Catch the Spirit" television program. They helped establish South Africa's first Emmaus Community.

Lydia J. Waters is pastor of the Enterprise United Methodist Church in Compton, California. Convenor of the Clergywomen's Association of the California-Pacific Conference, she is in great demand as a preacher throughout the country. She and her husband, Kenneth, are contributing editors for *Clergy Couples Connect* and were featured as a clergy couple on the "Catch the Spirit" television program. They helped establish South Africa's first Emmaus Community.

WHOM SHALL WE SEND?
An Introduction to the Debate

Donald E. Messer

Has a commitment to itineracy become the norm of faithfulness and obedience in United Methodism the way allegiance to biblical inerrancy has become the absolute test in some other denominations? Is it subversive activity if a person rejects possible appointments or raises questions about the viability, equity, or desirability of the traditional United Methodist way of deploying pastors to places of service? Does guaranteed appointment ensure mediocrity in ministry? Is it heretical to suggest that itineracy is already dead, or at least in the last stages of dying, and that the corpse is undermining the mission, ministry, and authority of the church? Or is the transformation of itineracy, yes, even the resurrection, still a possibility?

These are the kinds of questions laity and clergy are raising across the spectrum of United Methodism, as the church prepares for mission and ministry in the twenty-first century. This book affirms that while God calls persons to ministry, it is the responsibility of the whole church, both laity and clergy, to determine who is ordained and who will be sent to particular assignments. It is not just a matter for bishops or the clergy to decide, but for the whole people of God. Laity and clergy via their elected members of General Conference vote on legislation that sets the basic rules of itineracy. While laity do not vote at the final stages of the current ordination process, they are the first to vote on recommending clergy candidates from the local congregations.

An Invitation to Debate

The future system of deploying United Methodist clergy, therefore, will emerge from an informed debate that includes critical assessment of past history and current practices. Myths must be exposed, assumptions challenged, and options considered. Initially, itineracy was created and developed almost exclusively by single, white men (John Wesley married later, but his marriage would hardly be postulated as a model). Critiques by women and persons of color with distinct visions and differing values may create the possibility of alternatives embracing greater equity, justice, and humaneness.

Entrenched morphological fundamentalism—believing and/or acting as if the current system of organization and activity is divinely ordained and unchangeable—inevitably emerges when criticisms are leveled at the current system. Defensive mechanisms are triggered which limit imaginative consideration of how itineracy could be re-visioned. Discernment of what God wills for Christ's Church in the next millennium is often short-circuited because of our tendency to rely rigidly on past structures and systems.

This book seeks to provide a forum for thoughtful discussion of the basic questions and tensions facing the crisis in the United Methodist itineracy. Preferably, it presents the issues honestly and fairly, having neither a particular axe to grind nor an inordinate defensiveness about the current system. Its purpose is to encourage an intelligent debate within The United Methodist Church by providing needed historical and theological information and reflection about itineracy, descriptive data about how the system is working, critical perspectives and concerns that are authentic and often overlooked, as well as constructive suggestions worthy of future consideration.

To achieve these objectives a wide range of authors, lay and clergy, were invited to submit essays for this dialogue. Representative of the diversity of United Methodism, they have all experienced the values and dilemmas of itineracy. All clergy, whether now in local pastorates or in appointments beyond the local church or serving as bishops, have wrestled with a system that is built on the assumption that a person will go wherever he or she is sent. All have their own story of being appointed or sometimes being sent where they did not want to go. They know personally why itineracy has been known historically as a "system of sacrifice" and what the *The Book of Discipline* (par. 437) means when it says: "The itinerant system is the accepted method of The United Methodist Church by which ordained ministers are appointed by the bishop to fields of labor. All ordained ministers shall accept and abide by these appointments."

Redeeming and Renewing Itineracy

Lest this language give the impression or image of an all-powerful bishopric, it should be noted that many contemporary United Methodist bishops feel like Jonathan Swift's mythical traveler, Gulliver, pinned to the ground by hundreds of six-inch-tall Lilliputians in the form of regulations, consultations, demands, and expectations. In an earlier historical era, sole authority rested with the bishop to make or "fix" appointments, but in the contemporary church this power is shared to a degree because of consultation with the district superintendents, the local congregation, and the individual pastors involved. Like Gulliver, today's episcopal leaders often feel shackled by rules, overseers, paperwork, and procedures (not to mention potential legal hassles or caucus demands) that interrupt or interfere with their freedom to engage the church effectively in mission by making the best pastoral appointments.

Isaiah responded to the voice of God asking, "Whom shall I send, and who will go for us?" by exclaiming, "Here am I; send me!" (Isaiah 6:8 NRSV). The contemporary crisis facing itineracy may tempt United Methodist bishops to yearn for more Isaiah-like clergy who will respond to the question, "Whom shall I send and who will go for us?" by immediately and enthusiastically crying, "Here am I; send me!"

This response becomes more problematic, however, in a new context quite different from the circuit rider's American frontier. In an age of learned laity as well as learned clergy, neither is likely to welcome a rebirth of authoritarianism. Both are asking not only for a voice, but also for a choice, in decision making regarding appointments. In a time when both clergy and spouses may have professional identities and may feel economic pressures, arbitrary actions may not only disrupt callings and careers, but also destroy marriages and families. Clergy couples are committed to serving the church, but not if their relationship is broken by the pressure of living hundreds of miles apart.

The Council of Bishops has acknowledged the urgent need for re-visioning the United Methodist system of itineracy. In the Episcopal Address at the 1988 General Conference in St. Louis, the imperative of redeeming and renewing itineracy was affirmed.[1] The Commission for the Study of Ministry noted that "if itineracy is to remain a viable option for the church, issues of injustice and inequity, as well as accountability, availability, and authority must be addressed."[2]

The redemption and renewal of the itineracy, however, may mean something distinctly different to laity and clergy from what the bishops hope. Where you sit often determines where you stand. If you feel like Gulliver bound by "munchkins," then the idea of more consultation or a modified congregational connectionalism may be viewed as seriously detrimental to the denomination. If clergy or congregations feel as if they are oppressed by chains of injustice and inequity, then limiting episcopal powers and ensuring greater attention to special needs and considerations may be visualized as promising a more dynamic denomination.

On some of these issues a major perception gap may exist. For example, in the 1988 Episcopal Address clergy and spouses were told:

> We [the bishops] have a pastoral concern for the personal and family situations of all appointed clergy, yet if equity is to be restored and itineracy renewed, bishops and cabinets must insist that the minister who places personal and unofficial limits on itineracy can have no assurance of such limits being honored nor appointment within such limits guaranteed.[3]

Clergy and spouses, on the other hand, may feel that the episcopacy is neither giving their changing family situations appropriate attention nor showing sufficient sensitivity to the new professional and economic realities being experienced. What percentage of episcopal spouses are employed professionally outside the home? Do bishops have the same economic pressures? Are divorced pastors, who have limited visiting rights or share custody of their children, acting selfishly or being responsible Christians when they set limits on their itineracy? A "redeemed and renewed" itineracy requires more theological and sociological attention to the drastically changed family structures of contemporary and future United Methodist clergy.[4]

The Call, the Covenant, and Professionalism

United Methodists understand the ordained ministry to be more a calling than a career, more a covenant than a contract. Whereas the early circuit riders typically were unschooled enthusiasts, today's clergy tend to be well-educated, self-confident professionals. An unyielding appointment system may so frustrate some of the best and most promising pastors that they will choose to serve in other denominations. If decisions by those in authority are viewed as arbitrary, well-educated professionals may feel called to other paths of Christian service. A "redeemed and renewed" itineracy demands a reexamination of the meaning of Christian calling, a recovery of covenant relationships, and a review of professionalism.

Bishops report that more pastors are saying no when asked to take new appointments. Episcopal leaders struggle to find ways to be fair to clergy and their needs and yet simultaneously advance the mission of Christ. In the 1988 Episcopal Address they asked:

> Can the itineracy be renewed when considerable numbers of itinerant ministers declare themselves de facto non-itinerant? The answer must be no, because one of the assumptions of itineracy is equality of opportunity for every itinerant to serve in any place. But if all the places in what are deemed the more attractive locations are locked up by clergy who will serve only within a limited area, then the truly itinerant clergy are destined to serve out their lifetimes in less desirable places. Thus two classes of clergy are created, itinerant and non-itinerant, separate and unequal, with all of the advantages going to the non-itinerant.[5]

Critics respond, however, that equality of opportunity has certainly never existed for persons of color or for women. Large membership churches and their pastors have been treated in special ways. Clergy in appointments beyond the local church have experienced both advantages and disadvantages. Limited itineracy is not only the wave of the future, but the empirical reality of both the past and the present.

A seniority system has long prevailed. Clergy fresh out of seminary are often led to believe they can step on the bottom platform of an ecclesiastical escalator only to be carried upward toward some form of professional "success" with the passage of time. Their appointment is assured. Their advancement will be automatic. Thus, in some instances, Conference membership becomes a social security system for mediocrity. The triumph of the Peter Principle is almost guaranteed.

The seniority system often makes the pastor's salary a major criterion for a person's new appointment. Tragically, this may result in unfortunate "matches" between congregation and pastor. Episcopal leaders are conscious that the itineracy is being undermined by the "enormous disparity in salaries paid to pastors." They noted that

> we face a situation in some Annual Conferences where the setting of pastoral salaries is being used as a way to step out of the appointive system. Although the authority to set salary rests with the charge conference, the danger of a rampant congregationalism here must be recognized.[6]

The professional seniority system has encouraged a progressive rise in status and money over a period of time. Reflective of contemporary culture, clergy are tempted to expect the church to adjust to their personal desires and needs rather than expressing blind willingness to serve wherever they are sent.

These contrasting perceptions and positions necessitate increased dialogue regarding the call, the covenant, and professionalism. The journey of a connectional people may be calling forth new theological understandings and a reformed system of itineracy.

Historical Perspectives

Every debate on itineracy inevitably must be informed by an understanding of the history of this unique method of deploying pastors. Much misunderstanding can be clarified by an accurate account of how the system originated and developed.

Duke University historian Russell E. Richey could write an entire volume on the history of itineracy, but for purposes of this book his chapter, "Itineracy in Early Methodism," serves as a basic introduction to major events, themes, and developments. Special attention is given to changes in John Wesley's initial idea of itineracy. Richey asks, "If the character, performance, and health of the church are tied to itineracy . . . what happens to the church when itineracy changes?" He seriously questions whether the clock can be turned back and itineracy returned to an earlier day.

Providing an international Third World perspective is the Korean theologian and pastor Joon Kwan Un. "When Korea Abolished Guaranteed Appointments" reports on how a new era of phenomenal church growth developed. By viewing itineracy from the comparative vantage point of a context distinctly different from the United States, alternative possibilities and consequences can be imagined. Fearful of "local churchism" and longer pastorates becoming "lifelong pastorates," Un warns that connectionalism may be an endangered species in South Korea.

Foundational Perspectives

Dividing this book into sections tends to be somewhat theoretical and arbitrary. Every chapter in this book includes some historical references. Likewise they all might be considered foundational and challenging, since they are both appreciative and critical. Yet a case can be made that some of the authors tend to be more supportive of itineracy as now operative, while others are included who are less satisfied. While no writer is a blind apologist, chapters 3, 4, and 5, clearly are written by believing advocates.

Louisiana Bishop William B. Oden in "Without Reserve: A Critical Appreciation of the Itineracy" speaks of the values, strengths, and viability of the itinerant system. This foundational perspective outlines the official stance of the denomination, recognizing that the majority of United Methodists favor retaining some form of itineracy. By emphasizing the disciplinary mandate to offer oneself without reserve, Oden challenges the cultural tide of individualism. He believes that despite its weaknesses "itineracy is a part of God's plan of sharing the urgency of the good news of Jesus Christ with all people."

As a local pastor, M. Kent Millard affirms the foundational assumptions of itineracy but fears its spiritual dimensions have been lost to politics and pragmatism. He suspects everyone is consulted in the appointment process except God! In "Spiritual Discernment in Consultation" Millard recalls the devotional disciplines of John Wesley and proposes a model for making decisions that deliberately seek the will of God. Along with parish and pastor profiles, prayer becomes a priority in the appointment process.

As Associate General Secretary of the Board of Higher Education and Ministry, Donald H. Treese is committed to "Reaffirming the Covenant in Itineracy." He believes renewing the foundation of covenant relationships would resolve many problems besetting the ministry today, including the problem of ineffective pastors. Concerned that itineracy is becoming "just another management system," Treese underscores recovering the missional dimension of itineracy. Using comparisons with contemporary British Methodism, he struggles with the disparity of pastors' salaries.

Read together, these three essays by Oden, Millard, and Treese are foundational documents that articulate the basic dimensions and potentialities of itineracy as it functions in United Methodism today. Each raises probing questions and pressing criticisms, while at the same time affirming the imperative of itineracy for the church's future.

Challenging Perspectives

The next six chapters were written by authors who perceive the need for greater change in how itineracy currently operates. The challenges they raise can neither be ignored nor be resolved easily. They address systemic questions that are often overlooked or placed at the periphery by those responsible for decision making. These challenges strike at the heart of the future of itineracy and United Methodism.

Parish consultant and prolific author Lyle E. Schaller asks, "Who Is the Client?" as he questions whether itineracy is more beneficial for the clergy than for the church. Concerned with financial subsidies to small congregations via minimum salaries, Schaller challenges the "Robin Hood role" of the Annual Conference. The organizational structure of United Methodism has become dysfunctional. Calling for radical change, he questions guaranteed appointments, suggesting a possible phasing out of 17,000 clergy, and champions a greater congregational role in appointment making.

In "A Generic Lay Perspective," Iliff sociologist Sally B. Geis argues that itineracy may have once been appropriate to historical circumstances, but it is now ill-fitted to the contemporary context and needs. Challenging the "generic vision of clergy as appointable anywhere" she emphasizes cultural pluralism and the diversity of the denomination. The ethos of self-fulfillment for both laity and clergy must be respected. Fearful of abolishing guaranteed appointments, she is open to revising clergy compensation schemes, lest congregations bid "for star pastors the way big league franchises bid on star ball players."

Affirming the value and potentiality of connectionalism versus congregationalism are Bishop Susan M. Morrison and District Superintendent Gilbert H. Caldwell. In "Crossing Cultural, Racial, and Gender Boundaries" they endorse a missional emphasis of inclusiveness and encourage greater "open itineracy." They believe laity are less resistant than clergy and dare the church to blow the bugle of leadership.

Licensed psychologist Bonnie J. Messer and religious journalist Denise Johnson Stovall write as clergy spouses probing itineracy's utilitarian notion "which places the good of the larger church over the good of its individual members, in particular, the families of clergy." In "Conflicting Covenants: Clergy Spouses and Families" they highlight conflicting covenantal vows—marriage and ordination—and advocate a new understanding of vocation that respects the value and significance of dual career families. Psychological and ethical dimensions of itineracy are explored, and church leadership is challenged to embrace new sensitivities for clergy spouses and families.

Citing Priscilla and Aquila, the evangelist companions of Paul, as the earliest known prototypes of the clergy couple, Kenneth L. Waters and Lydia J. Waters explore the challenge of clergy couples to itineracy in "Married to the Church and to Each Other: Clergy Couples." As pastors serving local churches in California, they note that there are now more than nine hundred clergy couples in United Methodism. In fact, one-fourth of all clergywomen are part of a clergy couple. Asking whether clergy couples are a problem or a promise for itineracy, they articulate the major challenges posed and the changes needed. Quoting an old African-American adage, "if whites have a cold, we have the flu," they raise to consciousness particular concerns of global ethnic clergy and communities of faith.

"Liberation for a Culture in Crisis" by theologian Rebecca S. Chopp of Candler School of Theology at Emory University laments the loss to the church of many of the most talented clergy. Feminist and liberation theologians urge an itineracy that is demystified and reshaped to serve a culture in crisis. Clergy want a new sense of mission and ministry, a new vision and vocation. "Ministers," she claims, "are weary of the caretaking and management functions they have been assigned in the modern church."

Lifting Up Many Voices

Readers expecting or desiring a systematic critical and creative analysis of the variety of viewpoints expressed in these chapters are destined for a different experience. The editor seeks to lift up the many voices of United Methodism, but not prematurely to seek harmony amid discord. The purpose of this book is to advance the debate, not to orchestrate a grand finale or preconceived conclusion. These provocative essays from across the church are designed to stimulate imaginative and practical theological thinking. The future of an itineracy in crisis will evolve from the democratic dialogue and dissent of the denomination, as laity and clergy struggle with the issues and ideas spotlighted in these pages.

In the last chapter, "Where Do We Go From Here?" the editor offers his own perspective on the needed re-visioning of itinerant ministry, including a reassessment of basic assumptions, if the church and its clergy are to be revitalized for the twenty-first century. Bold and innovative and experimental thinking and strategies are encouraged, lest rigor mortis characterize United Methodism.

PART I: HISTORICAL AND THEOLOGICAL FOUNDATIONS

CHAPTER 1

Itineracy in Early Methodism

Russell E. Richey

"I am a travelling preacher of the Methodist persuasion, and have come in order to preach in this place." So Jesse Lee announced himself.[1] So Methodism introduced itself. So Methodism has understood itself—a movement led by wandering Arminians, traveling preachers.

> *Our grand plan,* in all its parts, leads to an *itinerant* ministry. Our bishops are *travelling* bishops. All the different orders which compose our conferences are employed in the *travelling line;* and our local preachers are, *in some degree,* travelling preachers. Every thing is kept moving as far as possible; and we will be bold to say, that, next to the grace of God, there is nothing *like this* for keeping the whole body alive from the center to the circumference, and for the continual extension of that circumference on every hand.[2]

About itinerants and itineracy, American Methodists have not been bashful. They have often taken itineracy to be the most distinctive and distinguishing feature of the movement.[3]

> The great, vital feature of the new church was its itinerant system. There had been itinerants before in the world's history, and missionaries of nearly every creed . . . but never before did a church destined to become great and powerful in the family of Christ establish as its main working force a body of men devoted to a perpetual pilgrimage, yet held strictly to the rules and discipline of ecclesiastical government.[4]

In itineracy Methodists gloried; in it they believed. Some thought it providential. "The *itinerant* system of preaching is of divine appointment, and unquestionably John Wesley, and his sons in the gospel, may justly claim in this respect to be in the *apostolic succession.*"[5] Others, less confident of its divinity, have been no less persuaded of its uniqueness, and, perhaps more important, of its centrality to Methodism.[6] For Gerald Kennedy, it was "the rock on which we have built our connectional system."[7] In 1843 *The Methodist Magazine* summarized its foundational character:

> The grand feature by which the polity of the Methodist Episcopal Church is characterized; that feature to which the others are in a great degree subordinate; and that feature which constitutes the main difference between ourselves and other evangelical denominations, is *an itinerating ministry*. From this arrangement flows the necessity of episcopacy, of conferences, of the office of presiding elders; and hence is perpetuated the unity of the church itself.[8]

If the character, performance, and health of the church are tied to itineracy as much as these citations would imply, what happens to the church when itineracy changes? United Methodism is, after all, a long way from the days indicated in the first *Minutes* by the stationing orders:

New York	Thomas Rankin	to change in
Philadelphia	George Shadford	four months.[9]

Has the itineracy transmuted itself into something else? Has it, for instance, become like the parish ministry of Wesley's day? Has Methodism lost that which distinguishes it? In answering such questions, we need to look at more than temporality and locality, though those will, in fact, be important considerations. Several contextual constellations gave itineracy its initial coloration and remain important in understanding its appearance in successive periods: (1) the social/cultural context within which Methodist ministry (itineracy) found itself, including the leadership styles prevalent in other denominations and the society at large; (2) the web of other Wesleyan practice (e.g., connection, appointment, superintendency) in its current expression, meaning, and operation; (3) the leadership structure of the movement, and in particular the way functions and roles were differentiated and allocated on the local level; (4) the rhythms, calendar, and geography of the movement.[10]

If we take only the last, we might move quickly to remark how a mobile office became stationary, how a national ministerium became local, how an extraordinary office became ordinary, but that oversimplifies the story.

Itineracy in Social Context

In Britain, George Whitefield's and John Wesley's practice of itinerant preaching and Wesley's regularization of it into a precept for ministerial order broke with both custom and law. The established church functioned with offices graded like the chain of being from national down to parish level, each geographically defined. The parish priest or curate was a communal figure, a leader whose whole career might well be exercised in one town or in one parish of a city and whose work was confined therein. Reinforcing that medieval pattern, by Wesley's day, were the memories and experiences with Puritanism, attitudes codified in the so-called Clarendon Code, which proscribed enthusiasm and set very narrow limits for non-Anglican or dissenting religious practice, limits that Wesley successfully defied, but limits that nonetheless affected how both he and the society viewed what he was about. Recognizing its deviance from established patterns, Wesley termed the ministry of his itinerants "extraordinary," a designation he defined theologically, as we shall see in a moment, but which had ecclesiastic and social force as well. Itineracy was quite irregular; it did not belong; it violated communal norms. In New England, also, as Whitefield's example proved, the vernacular and itinerant style violated custom, elicited imitators and unleashed new patterns of religious leadership and communication.[11]

Itineracy frequently has been seen in old or New England perspective, an appropriate viewpoint given both Methodist origins and the terrific conflict into which Methodism plunged in the early nineteenth century when it penetrated Calvinist Congregationalist strongholds. By happenstance, early Methodist historians—notably Jesse Lee and Nathan Bangs—played key roles in the conflict with Congregationalism. They viewed itineracy as unique and in contrast to an essentially congregational norm. However, that perspective, though illuminating, may not be the most accurate or helpful portrayal of American reception of and reaction to Methodist itinerants. Early American Methodism was primarily a movement of the Chesapeake, middle colonies, and upper South, not of the North.[12]

In those contexts, itineracy was a way of life necessitated by widespread settlements, very few settled clergy, religious and linguistic diversity, and parishes or areas of religious responsibility defined in square miles, not by village squares. The grand itinerant George Whitefield served as the model for some of that itinerating, but much emerged spontaneously as scattered settlements cried for religious service and the few available clergy responded.[13] Similar itinerating patterns among the Reformed, Lutherans, Presbyterians, Mennonites, Moravians, and other Pietist groups—undertaken often in response to desperate pleas from leaderless communities—produced the widespread religious ferment, organization, and excitement identified as the Middle Atlantic phase of the Great Awakening.[14]

The earliest itineracy among groups that now constitute United Methodism probably occurred in such spontaneous fashion among those communities that coalesced into the United Brethren. Philip William Otterbein and Martin Boehm both traveled to conduct services and to meet the various religious needs of scattered Reformed and Mennonite communities. In addition, Boehm used the established pattern of great meetings, like Methodist quarterly meetings and later camp meetings, to aggregate thinly settled believers into an assembly that met for several days for preaching.[15] Before British Methodism made its entry, even before the unappointed lay pioneers initiated Methodist preaching, itineracy was an American and a German "Methodist" practice.

Methodists, thanks to Mr. Wesley, put into precept, pattern, and policy what for others had been only practice. In reflecting on itineracy, Methodists rightly refer to Wesley. His program, and not the existing but inchoate colonial practice, defined early American Methodism. Indeed, the earliest preachers show virtually no awareness of prior itineracy, save that of Whitefield. Its theory originated with Wesley. Yet its prevalence in the colonies contributed to the success that Methodist itineracy enjoyed and the reception that it found. It was already ordinary, not extraordinary, customary not abnormal, a practice if not a precept.

When we look at itineracy from the perspective of those who lived in the Chesapeake area, rather than New England, we see that from the start Methodist ministry closely approximated existing cultural styles. In the decades and centuries after 1784, Methodist itineracy continued to look remarkably like ministry in other communions and indeed like the leadership patterns exercised generally in

American history.[16] In each period of ministry, the Methodist itinerant closely resembled his or her counterpart in other Protestant denominations. Itineracy found some way of accommodating the remarkable changes in tenure, role, self-understanding, training, function, and status through which American ministry has evolved. That evolution also approximated significant stages in the leadership of American society—booster in the early nineteenth century, cultured communal elite in the latter nineteenth, progressive or prophetic reformer in the early twentieth, corporate manager up through the 1950s, and more recently medical-style professional.[17] Through these various metamorphoses, Methodists continued to speak of their ministry as itinerating. However, with each adaptation, the meaning of itineration changed significantly.

The cultural adaptation of itineracy has produced two dominant assessments: first, one valuing positively the consequent increase of freedom, democracy, inclusiveness, consultation, and lay prerogative;[18] and second, one viewing the dramatic changes as having fundamentally violated Methodist principle. In adjudicating that debate we need to look at other indices of Methodist change. We also should note, though we cannot explore the point fully here, that in the interaction with culture, Methodism contributed as well as received, shaping the culture as well as influencing it, a point suggestively elaborated by Nathan O. Hatch and a recurrent theme in Methodist treatment of itineracy.[19] In particular, Methodist ministry resembled that of other Protestant leadership because other Protestants mimicked the Methodists, especially in the nineteenth century and in the conquest of the frontier for which itineracy proved the premier form of evangelization.[20]

Itineracy in Wesleyan Context

Though Methodist ministry has resembled that of other communions more than Methodists have sometimes wanted to admit, itineracy was nonetheless characteristically and unmistakably Wesleyan. Itinerants were initially, in both Britain and America, "extraordinary messengers"; persons gifted in the Spirit to preach scriptural Christianity; Wesley's sons in the gospel; chosen by, directed by, and accountable to him; under appointment sent to a circuit and to travel that circuit; bound together with other such helpers into the connection and in recognition of Wesley's superintendence over them and the people called Methodist.[21] They were explicitly not ordinary ministers—that is, not appointed to administer sacraments, not ordained to the priestly office, not parish-bound.[22] Wesley outlined their nature and tasks in *The Large Minutes:*

> Q. 24 In what view must we and our *Helpers* be considered?
> A. Perhaps as Extraordinary Messengers (i.e. out of the ordinary way) designed 1. To provoke the regular Ministers to jealousy. 2. To supply their lack of service, toward those who are perishing for want of knowledge.
> Q. 25 What is the Office of an *Helper?*
> A. In the absence of a Minister, to feed and guide the flock: In particular, 1. To preach Morning and Evening. . . . 2. To meet the Society and the Bands weekly. . . . 3. To meet the Leaders weekly. . . .[23]

Itineracy was, then, defined by its relation to Wesley (the appointive power), through its purposes and over against parish ministry, but ostensibly within the Church of England. It was extraordinary.

In 1784 itineracy changed in essence, though not initially in manifestation. As an episcopal church, American Methodism now offered the ordinary ministrations—most notably the sacraments—but also those offices and functions that fall to presbyters and for which Methodists had previously resorted to the parish church. Fittingly, the new church recognized its ministry with proper ecclesial titles—deacon, elder, and bishop (initially superintendent). The church retained the Wesleyan procedures and terminology—the distinction between traveling and local preachers, admission on trial, conference membership—juxtaposing the ecclesial and the Wesleyan, the ordinary and the extraordinary and leaving the integration of elder with traveling preacher and the relation of deacon to "on trial" to be worked out. The meshing of those offices and functions took time, as the next section will indicate, a process completed only as stations displaced circuits and Methodism made the former its norm.[24] Nevertheless, we need to underscore the obvious point—namely, that Wesleyan itineracy had not been designed to bear the ordinary offices and to serve the congregational needs that over two centuries it increasingly assumed. (German Methodists, less reliant upon Wesley and heirs to ecclesial principles from the Lutheran and Reformed traditions, seemed less troubled by this puzzle.[25])

Developments in appointment and connection corresponded to

changes in itineracy. Indeed, itineracy at any point in time is intelligible only in relation to these other Wesleyan essentials. They, too, defined the "extraordinary" office and were gradually and subtly altered by the assumption of "ordinary" episcopal and ecclesial roles. The appointive power was one that itineracy and itinerants knew well. Francis Asbury summed up ministry under the appointive power in his 1813 Valedictory: "It is the traveling apostolic order and ministry that is found in our very constitution. . . and all are movable at the pleasure of the superintendent whenever he may find it necessary for the good of the cause."[26] In accepting the call to itinerate, the prospective minister placed himself (and not until the mid-twentieth century herself) at the disposal of the connection, to be sent where the bishop and those who shared in the bishop's appointive functions, the presiding elders and those in charge of circuits, determined. Self-sacrifice and obedience were requisite:

> When a man takes upon himself the obligations of a Methodist preacher he identifies himself with the system. The question is not, then, whether he will go to this or that appointment, but whether he will hereafter obey the voice of the Church, and go to such fields of labor as the judgment of its constituted authorities may determine. . . . This mode of making appointments is called by some *the tyranny* of the system. If so, it is a tyranny that each one voluntarily assumes, and with which he voluntarily remains.[27]

Methodist preachers knew their ministry and that of the connection to be determined by that appointive power. Complaints about the exercise of that power recur through our history. Virtually every political fracas and division has, at one level or another, challenged episcopal authority, some explicitly like the Republican Methodists, the Methodist Protestants, and the Free Methodists, others implicitly. Though the basic issue was slavery, the split in 1844 also turned on the nature and exercise of the appointive power. The exercise and evolution of the episcopal office play a central part in the story of itineracy, a point to which we will return briefly.

In theory, bishops made appointments in the interest of the connection (though that fact was not always obvious to those sent or to the receiving charge). The connection, originally those literally in connection with Mr. Wesley, took social form in America in a hierarchy of conferences, each responsible with the appointive authority, for the ministry of a given area. The most basic, though not the smallest, of these was the Annual Conference, which eventually stabilized as the Methodist counterpart to a state. In a particular conference, the traveling preachers held their membership. Conference became family, fraternity, and community for the preachers. Jesse Lee's account of his first conference in 1782, a gathering of some thirty preachers, illustrates the great intensity of the bond:

> The union and brotherly love which I saw among the preachers, exceeded every thing I had ever seen before, and caused me to wish that I was worthy to have a place amongst them. When they took leave of each other, I observed that they embraced each other in their arms, and wept as though they never expected to meet again. Had the heathens been there, they might have well said, "see how these Christians love one another!" By reason of what I saw and heard during the four days that the conference sat, I found my heart truly humbled in the dust, and my desires greatly increased to love and serve God more perfectly than I had ever done before.[28]

Two aspects of this conference gathering deserve comment. First, the intense fraternal display defined a community, a body of preachers, who labored together to serve the connection. Lee entered a collective service which, as E. Dale Dunlap indicates, functioned as a covenant between the body of preachers and the Methodist societies, a covenant mediated by the appointing power.[29] As Bishops Asbury and Coke explained, itinerants served, deliberated, and acted, for "the good of the whole," with "an enlarged, apostolic spirit, which would endeavour, whatever might be the sacrifice, to make all things *tally*."[30] Preachers dramatized and experienced the corporate character of that sacrificial service in conference gatherings.

Second, conference was and remained through much of the nineteenth century a very intense fraternal experience. Much of its intensity derived from conference's inquiry into the character, gifts, belief, and religious experience of its members—those being received on trial and continued on trial and those under appointment. Methodists understood and conducted those processes as the exercise of discipline, understood themselves to be under discipline, understood itineracy to be a disciplined life.[31] The disciplined life and the disciplining of those who failed to live it, employing trials as the last resort, gets frequent treatment in discussions of itineracy. Here we would remark on its ordinary power, the way that the intense scrutiny produced fraternal (male) bonding, camaraderie, and family feeling. Initially conducted in camera the review of character functioned to build close relations among the preachers and to make conference a covenanted community.[32]

Intimacy and bonding came also from traveling together, a practice far more common than our image of the lonely itinerant would suggest, and undertaken routinely in the apprenticing of new itinerants, as the following account by William Burke indicates:

> In the fall, at the beginning of October, brother Lowe insisted that I should accompany him round New Hope circuit. Accordingly, I arranged my business so as to make the tour of six weeks. We went on together, preaching time about, till he was taken sick and returned home, and left me to complete the round.[33]

The bonds were cemented by such shared apprenticing experience, as well as by common adversity and a common wage, by the peculiar transitory relation they enjoyed with the Methodist people, by the equally peculiar continuing relation they enjoyed with the appointive power, by the stories they shared, by correspondence, and by the intense engagement with each other in conference.[34] Itinerants traveled a common road, both metaphorically and literally.

Male bonding has negative as well as positive features. Fraternal feeling among the brethren doubtless explains, in some measure, the difficulty white preachers found in accepting their black "brethren" into full membership, the necessity they found for separating out ministries to linguistic and ethnic groups into separate conferences, and later the great resistance they showed in recognizing the call to preach that women experienced.[35] In fact, women did preach and did itinerate, in both Wesley's England and Asbury's America[36] but were not accorded until well into the twentieth century full standing in the "traveling" ministry.

Fraternity was then vulnerable to the various ills that beset human community, including prejudice, short-sightedness, and self-interest. It proved especially vulnerable to aging, death, conflict, growth, novelty, and social change. Though a sense of "brotherhood" continues to this day—despite the radical pluralization of ministry, the admission of women into the ranks of the ordained, and the transformation of conference from a preacher's order into a body with roughly equal proportions of clergy and laity—conference has changed radically and with it the Wesleyan context for ministry. Very early the fraternity gathered to itself legislative and judicial functions and around the mid-nineteenth century conference had become a political entity. Conference's political potentialities were especially sharpened by the conflicts over the reform movement that resulted in Methodist Protestantism and over slavery and abolition. Pressures for lay and female participation furthered that political development. In the early twentieth century, conference took on certain features of the modern corporation, as did the denomination as a whole. In the middle decades of the century, conferences increasingly behaved like professional societies, and like the A.M.A or A.B.A., though on regional rather than national levels, concerned themselves with matters of professional status, credentialing, salary, authority, competence, and prerogative. The evolution of conference and the connectional principle affected and was effected by the evolution of itineracy.

So also the evolution of the appointive power, of the episcopacy, affected and was effected by the changes in itineracy. For instance, both episcopacy and itineracy, once national in character, gradually became parochial offices. The bishops remained itinerating general superintendents in theory and self-understanding, but found themselves made first sectional and then, in the twentieth century, virtually provincial officers. The limitations put on episcopal horizons accelerated the collapse of itineracy from a national to a conference ministry.

The national character of early itineracy was well illustrated by Thomas Ware of New Jersey. Converted in Mount Holly (c. 1780), he became active in filling appointments on that circuit. Asbury sent him in 1783 to Dover circuit as an assistant. He attended the spring and Christmas conferences of 1784, while serving the year in Kent, located on the eastern shore of Maryland. The years following found him at Salem, New Jersey (1785), Long Island (1786), Holston (1787), East New River (1788), Caswell, North Carolina (1789), Wilmington, Delaware (1791), and Staten Island, New York (1792). The next year he became a presiding elder, an office he held until 1808, at Susquehanna (1793), Albany (1794), Philadelphia (1796), Peninsula (1800), Philadelphia (1802), New Jersey (1803), and again Philadelphia districts. Supernumerary in 1809 and superannuated in 1810, he returned later for active work in Lancaster and Long Island.[37]

Asbury valued such national appointments and warned in his Valedictory "against the growing evil of locality in bishops, elders, preachers, or Conferences."[38] Asbury's warning could not withstand the variety of forces that impelled the church toward confining itineracy within conference. The reasons included the sectional spirit of the land, the geographical stabilization of conferences, the marriages of itinerants, and a delegated and elective General Conference, which put a premium on nurturing a conference constituency. The result was that a national ministerium became parochial. A further consequence, according to both nineteenth-century contemporaries and twentieth-century interpreters, was civil war.[39]

Leadership Structure

Itineracy was defined by its place in the leadership structure of the movement, and in particular by the way ministerial functions and roles were differentiated and allocated on the local level. In the earliest years, the defining relationships were the presiding elder on one side and the local pastor and class leader on the other.

The presiding elder emerged in the late 1780s[40] as an extension of the appointive office with jurisdictional charge over the circuits gathered into a district. However, from the start and by Wesley's intention, the eldership functioned ordinarily as well. For instance, initially the few ordained as elders circulated to celebrate the sacraments.[41] In both their extraordinary and ordinary capacities, the presiding elders fulfilled or completed the local ministerial office.

The fulfillment and completion occurred most clearly and dramatically at quarterly meeting (quarterly conference). Those two-day dramas had become great religious festivals, intense revivalistic occasions, well before 1784. At them (after the 1780s) and with the presiding elder "presiding," the circuit did its extraordinary business, including reckoning financial accounts; scrutinizing class leaders, stewards, exhorters, local preachers, and those who had begun to travel; exercising discipline, including hearing appeals from class and society cases; overseeing "the spiritual and temporal business of the societies in his district";[42] in short, exercising "within his own district, during the absence of the superintendents, all the powers invested in them for the government of our church."[43] Quarterly meetings performed ordinarily as well. They gathered large crowds, particularly for the third quarter, in late summer, and offered the full range of religious services, including love feasts, preaching, the Lord's Supper, and baptism or memorial services as appropriate.

Quarterly Meetings

The 1788 report by Robert Ayers was entirely typical, save for the presence of Asbury:

Saturday, July 26th: We held a Quarterly Meeting, and I suppose there were not less than one thousand people there. I opened the Meeting with an exhortation, and Brother Conaway followed with another, and then Mr. Asbury preached from Revelation 3:20, and Brother Whatcoat followed with an exhortation, and then Brother Phoebus concluded.

Sunday, July 27th: We held a love feast early in the morning. At ten o'clock Brother Matthews began with an exhortation, and Brother Lurton and Brother Simmons followed. Then Mr. Asbury preached, and Brother Whatcoat concluded. Then the ordination of a Deacon and the administration of the Lord's Supper was performed. I tarried at the Widow Murphys.[44]

At the quarterly meetings both the extraordinary (itinerant) and ordinary (sacramental) offices were completed or fulfilled by the presiding elder or, at least, under the presidency of the presiding elder. In the early nineteenth century, the church found a vehicle for that completion of ministry—namely, the camp meeting. Thereafter, presiding elders appointed quarterly meetings for camp meetings.

The itinerant anticipated and depended on such occasions for a range of ministerial functions that he did not or could not perform as he made his two-week or four-week or six-week circuit. The camp meeting became a stable and popular aspect of Methodist ministry. So that dependence was not resisted; it was rather by design and by *Discipline.* That dependence existed whether the itinerant in question was on trial, a deacon, or an elder. Still, the presiding elder crowded the itinerant from the top, as it were.

The crowding lessened dramatically when the itinerants assumed stations. Then preachers, typically elders, routinely performed the offices, both ordinary and extraordinary, that had earlier awaited the quarterly meeting and the gathering of the circuits. They did so because they remained present through the week and from week to week and were therefore able to deal with the congregation's various religious needs, ordinary and extraordinary. Bangs celebrated this development:

Whatever may be said against this policy in other parts of our work, it is certain that its adoption in many portions of the country in the eastern and northern states has had a beneficial influence upon the interests of our Church. By this means the people have been able to meet the expense of sustaining the worship of God, and also to secure permanent congregations; and the preachers could more fully and effectually discharge *all* the duties of pastors, in overseeing the temporal and spiritual affairs of the Church, such as visiting from

> house to house, attending upon the sick, burying the dead, meeting the classes, and regulating sabbath school, tract, and missionary societies. And who will say that these things are not as important to the well-being of the Church, or the prosperity of true religion, as it is "to preach so many sermons?[45]

For the panoply of pastoral offices, stations did not need to wait for a presiding elder every quarter since they had an elder on site. For stations, quarterly meetings became occasions for the connection to intrude on congregational life and the congregation to honor its connection. Quarterly conference or charge conference remained important connectional events, but they no longer crowded, completed, or fulfilled the ministry as they had for circuits.

Similarly, itineracy depended on the offices "below" it. In the earliest period, both the class leader and the local preacher functioned very much like the parson of Wesley's England or the parish minister in contemporary United Methodism. They served local ministerial needs, whether appointed to do such according to disciplinary procedure, by default, or through community request. They often initiated and typically sustained the ministry on the local level.

Local preachers proved to be an immensely important cog in the Methodist machinery. A stable office in the received Wesleyan order, exercised under the traveling preacher's authority, ordained to deacon by 1789, regulated by a distinct disciplinary paragraph by 1796, and in 1812 made eligible for elder's orders,[46] the local ministry was a point of entry to itineracy for some, a permanent local office for others and, perhaps most important, the station to which traveling preachers, unable or unwilling to itinerate, resorted. The latter category included some of the most able of the itinerants, many choosing not to travel and to leave the conference after marriage.[47] Asbury complained repeatedly that marriage ruined Methodist ministry: "Marriage is honourable in all—but to me it is a ceremony awful as death. Well may it be so, when I calculate we have lost the travelling labours of two hundred of the best men in America, or the world, by marriage and consequent location."[48] For much of our history, the local ministry also outnumbered the traveling, three to one according to Jesse Lee in 1799,[49] 850 local to 269 traveling, maintaining that proportion in 1812 according to Bishop McKendree, and slipping to two to one by the 1830s.[50]

The local ministry affected and, one might say, defined itineracy. In part, it did so by its sheer numbers. More important, until the itinerants began to settle into stations, the local minister provided for congregational needs. A good illustration is provided by Mudge of his own kinsman, Enoch Mudge, who after traveling with Lee and supervising Maine for six months in 1796, located at Orrington in 1799 "where he had married two years before."

> He remained there eighteen years. He became at once the teacher of the winter school (for a long time the only one in the place), he was the local pastor, whoever might be the circuit preacher, he administered the sacraments, solemnized marriages, and conducted funerals throughout the surrounding country, and was emphatically *the* man of the whole region, sent repeatedly to the Legislature at Boston, and looked up to as one of the fathers of the town, although still young, so that his name became a household word there for a generation following.[51]

Essentially the same point has been made by Norwood on the relation of class leader to itinerant. When the traveling preacher really traveled, the community relied on class leaders for local ministerial needs. "The class leader was needed to perform those pastoral functions which are part of a balanced ministry. But when the preacher settled down in a parsonage as a stationed pastor, the class leader (and along with him the local preacher and exhorter) became, at least so it seemed, an unnecessary wheel."[52]

There were interesting ironies and real tensions in the relations between the itinerant and the local officers, as well as between the itinerant and the presiding elder. The itinerant performed extraordinarily, to use Wesley's term, but possessed according to the *Discipline* some authority for and oversight of the ordinary pastoral duties. The local preacher, class leader, exhorter, and stewards performed ordinarily, but lacked full authority and conference membership. Not surprisingly, the church felt pressures for local preacher and lay participation in Annual Conference, pressures that affected the reform movement and the emergence of Methodist Protestantism.

A similar set of ironies and tensions characterized the relation between the itinerant and the presiding elder. The traveling preacher might be in charge, on both extraordinary and ordinary levels, but yielded to the presiding elder at quarterly meeting time when the business of the circuit would be completed and many of the ordinary ecclesial rituals performed. This pressure also vented itself politically in the debates over election of the presiding elders.

These tensions were not entirely resolved, but they were reframed when the itinerant did settle. Then, the so-called traveling preacher exercised the ordinary functions, offering those on a more regular basis than quarterly and, in so doing, preempted the roles previously played by local preacher and class leader. The settling into ordinary functions occurred at different rates in different places through the latter half of the nineteenth and early twentieth centuries. So Methodist ministry reconfigured itself and reimaged itself in terms of the new set of "ordinary" parish duties. However, it continued to be defined by its place in the leadership structure of the movement, and in particular by the way ministerial functions and roles were differentiated and allocated on the local level. Ministry reflected the new structures that emerged during that period and the roles played by both men and women in the Sunday school, missionary society, temperance organization, and the various congregational offices.

The "location" of the itinerant raised questions then, and it raises questions now about the extraordinary purposes for which Wesley intended the office. To understand that we need to conclude with a few statements concerning the temporal and spatial changes in itineracy.

The Rhythms, Calendar, and Geography of Itineracy

"All the Preachers to change at the end of 6 months," the *Minutes* stipulated in 1774, an expectation reiterated in 1794.[53] They experimented with quarterly changes as well. The terms gradually lengthened.[54] What had been an extraordinary ministry—a regimen suited for young, unmarried, mobile, healthy men, to be deployed on a national basis and moved frequently—evolved slowly in ordinary directions. The evolution had something to do with the changing Methodist calendar, as quarterly, biannual, annual, biennial, triennial, quadrennial, and eventually variable terms became the norm. The length of terms and the debates on setting or lengthening them focused the church's concerns about the change in its ministry. The changes were indeed quite dramatic. United Methodist theological students and conference personnel now speak about parish ministry as *the* norm with no sense of the ambiguity and irony inherent in that self-description. The rhythms and geography of today's ministry differ radically from that of early American Methodism or of Wesley's England. Today the clergy look much more like the parish parsons of Wesley's day than his itinerants.

Yet before United Methodists focus on some aspect of change as the culprit—perhaps now on the required "consultation"—they should consider how much the dramatic alterations were prefigured by the decisions made in 1784, how closely the evolution tracks that of other American denominational clergy, styles of secular leadership, and how the changes in itineracy cohere with those in the overall leadership structure. Reformers often wish to turn back the clock and recover the vitalities of an earlier day, certainly a laudable and, in some instances, effective ploy. The appeal to the past can indeed focus issues about the nature and purpose of the church and its ministry. Before we focus on itineracy or some aspect thereof that should be returned to the style of Wesley or Asbury or some latter day, we should remind ourselves that the clock has run also on the several contexts within which itineracy defines itself. American ministry has changed; the web of other Wesleyan practice has changed; the leadership structure of the movement has changed. Itineracy cannot be returned to an earlier day, at least not without corresponding societal, ecclesial, and administrative reversals.

More needful than hindsight is a compelling vision for the future. In that, the memory of our itinerant fathers and mothers should figure. Memory, including the memory of our own tradition, constitutes an important source of Methodism's self-understanding, a point reinforced in the *Discipline*'s Theological Guidelines and its appeal to history.[55] We do need to be reminded of our forebears' visions *and* their perplexities, which can provide a stimulus for today's ministry. However, it will not suffice. History can inform but not provide the vision.

CHAPTER 2

When Korea Abolished Guaranteed Appointments

Joon Kwan Un

The dramatic growth of Korean Methodism since 1978 is surely a surprising phenomenon to those who are within the particular family, as well as to fellow Methodists throughout the world. In contrast to the critical situation that prevails in The United Methodist Church, especially with the decline in membership since the early 1960s, the Korean Methodist Church's growth is undoubtedly miraculous.[1]

However, the tragic experience of Korean Methodism, often ignored amid the praise for numerical growth, needs to be appreciated. In reality, Korean Methodism has suffered long internal and factional conflicts and divisions, which, according to historical research, have been caused mainly by the episcopacy and the appointment system. As a consequence, Korean Methodism had only 600,000 members in 1978 while the Korean Presbyterian Church, which has the same length history as Methodism, had achieved a membership of 2,400,000.[2]

The scope of our discussion here, however, will be confined to two major areas of concern. The first is to explain why the episcopacy and the appointment system of Korean Methodism contributed to hindering church growth until 1978. The second is to interpret the miraculous events affecting church growth and the transformation of the Korean Methodist Church after the appointment system was abolished in 1978.

The Abolition of the Appointment System

The abolition of the appointment system in Korea was not a single day's event that simply abandoned what is called "connectionalism." Rather, it came as a necessity in 1978 when Korean Methodism was forced to consider either reunion or separation of the two split bodies. At this point we examine the tragic elements of division and search for the internal factors that caused the rupture in the course of the church's history.

The Birth of the Autonomous Korean Methodist Church in 1930. The first period (from 1885, the year Korean Methodism started, to 1930, when the autonomous Korean Methodist Church was born) was an era of great spiritual, political, and cultural awakening of the Korean people as a whole, who were oppressed by the Japanese invasion and who were abandoned and ignored by the international political community. The mission of the Korean Methodist Church was the transformation of the people, society, and culture of Korea, which was carried out rather successfully, mainly by American missionaries. The itineracy system was successful because it had been a tradition of the Methodist Church and "itinerant preachers served the people under the conditions where a settled ministry was not feasible,"[3] as described in *The Book of Discipline.*

The most significant historical event, as far as Korean Methodism is concerned, was the birth of the autonomous Korean Methodist Church on December 2, 1930, at the first General Conference, which was attended by about 100 delegates. Bishop Herbert Welch, then resident Bishop of Korea, officially pronounced the union of the two Methodist churches in Korea, which were related to the northern and southern Methodist churches in the United States. In doing so he declared the new Korean Methodist Church to be a "true Christian," "true Methodist," and "true Korean" Church. This event preceded the 1939 reunion of the American Methodist churches by nine years.[4]

C. A. Sauer, a lifelong missionary to Korea and interpreter of the living story of Korean Methodism, characterized six subsequent changes following the union and called these changes the democratization of church government.[5] It was democratic enough to have limited the episcopal term to four years with one reelection, to have included maximum lay participation in the policy-making processes at every level, and to have adopted an electoral system in which district superintendents were to be elected rather than appointed by the bishop.[6] The electoral system, though democratic in its nature, would become the root of confusion and tension between the episcopacy and the local church pastors in the years that followed.

Three more changes at the union event of 1930 contributed to the formation of democratic church government. The "Korean Creed" was adopted for the education of the congregation, women were honored as eligible for ordination, and the two ordinations, deacon and elder, were integrated into a single ordination called "moksa" (pastor). However, the itineracy and the appointment system continued in this period without any challenge.

Episcopacy Declines and Korean Methodism Suffers Under Japanese Oppression (1939–1945). The most troubled and confused time of Korean Methodism came after the election of Bishop Choon Soo Chung, a mere puppet of the Japanese policy, when he was installed as "Tong-Ni" (Director-General) of the Korean Methodist Church. During his dictatorial rule, Bishop Chung prohibited the use of the Old Testament and the book of Revelation in worship services, closed thirty-six Methodist churches, and barred from the pulpit many pastors who were known to be pro-American and anti-Japanese.

Bishop Chung's abuse of episcopal power lowered church membership to the bottom, broke down any possible credibility and literally rendered Korean Methodism dead.[7] Bishop Chung remains a nightmare to many Methodists, who consider his episcopacy the source of the evil root of conflicts and divisions in subsequent years. From then on the authority of the bishop's power and the appointment system were questioned.

Four Tragic Divisions and Reunion (1946–1978). As the Korean people celebrated the rebirth of their nation, Korean Methodism split into two groups. Those who supported Bishop Chung called themselves the "Bok Heung Pa" (Revival Group) and remained in the churches as pastors. But those who opposed the bishop's policy named their group the "Jae Kun Pa" (Reconstruction Group). It is ironic that while Korean Presbyterianism split between those who had worshiped at the Shinto shrine and those who had refused, Korean Methodists divided into those who had supported the "undue cooperation with and subservience to the police system"[8] of Bishop Chung and those who had opposed it. It was a great day for the Methodists when the divided groups finally reunited after long negotiations, and a new bishop, the Reverend Yoo Soon Kim, was elected. Unfortunately, the wounds of distrust remained unhealed.

The second division occurred in 1951 when Bishop Hyungki Lew, who had once opposed Bishop Chung and was expelled by him in turn, was elected to the episcopacy by an overwhelming vote. This time those who supported Chung felt defeated and walked out, organizing a separate body called the "Ho Hun Pa" (Group for

Defense of the Constitution). Another reconciliation between the two groups was achieved in 1958 when a new bishop, J. P. Kim, was elected. The third separation for just about the same reason took place from 1970 through 1974. While the vicious cycle of separation and reunion continued, the authority of the bishop declined, and church growth remained static.

The most critical division troubled the Korean Methodist Church in 1974 when forty delegates to the General Conference walked out in the middle of the sessions in protest against the most corrupt electoral system ever manipulated for the election of an all-powerful bishop. Those who walked out organized what was called the "Renewal General Conference," while the ones who remained elected a new bishop, the Reverend Chang H. Kim, immediately after the forty delegates left.

I was at that time the senior minister of historic Chung Dong First Methodist Church in Seoul, the oldest church of Methodism in Korea, and was caught in the middle between two radically opposed groups. I was privileged under the guidance of the Holy Spirit to serve as mediator between the hostile groups in the last hours of reunion talks. It was a very sad experience to see the wounds so deeply rooted in the minds of Korean Methodists who had lost confidence and trust in the office of bishop and in the appointment system, which had played an oppressive role instead of carrying out a ministry of service.

After a long struggle of talks between the two groups, a final plan for reunion was agreed upon through *four principles:*[9] (1) the creation of a council of bishops (election of multiple bishops instead of a single bishop); (2) autonomous operation and professionalization of each board; (3) local congregation and local church-centered structure (abolition of appointment system); and (4) new system of electing delegates to the General Conference. (Ministers with full connection for ten years or more automatically become delegates. Lay delegates are elected in the same number as ministerial delegates.)

On October 26, 1978 the Korean Methodist Church celebrated its reunion which brought the two hostile friends together, its new structure which elected four new bishops by the votes of delegates who were no longer chosen politically, its new policy which set forth a campaign program for "5,000 churches and one million members," and its new spirit which called the church to be in mission and service to the world. An entirely new Korean Methodism was born, marking a new beginning and a new mission.

Significant Phenomena After 1978

Two distinct dimensions of change became apparent after the appointment system was abolished in 1978. One dimension was the quantitative growth of church membership and churches, and the other dimension might be called the qualitative and communal transformation of the Methodist Church.

Statistics of Church Growth[10]

1. Membership Growth

Year	Members	
1908	37,030	
1918	26,338	(due to Japanese oppression)
1928	25,295	
1930	46,492	(the year the autonomous Methodist Church was born)
1936	54,636	
1951	45,716	(due to divisions and conflicts)
1958	268,165	(war experience drove people into faith and refugees from North were added)
1968	261,701	(conflicts continued because of the appointment system)
1978	597,691	(the appointment system gradually lost its validity and the local churches were given power to choose pastors)
1990	1,125,667	(12 years after the appointment system was abolished)

2. Number of Churches[11]

Year	Churches
1978	2,000
1986	2,832
1990	3,645

These statistics show that the membership of Korean Methodism nearly doubled in the twelve years after the great reunion as the local church-centered structure took effect in 1978. Likewise, the number of churches increased almost twice during the same period after the pastors became more responsible to the congregation than to the episcopal office.

The Qualitative and Communal Transformation of Korean Methodism Since the Great Reunion of 1978. One of the most striking changes in pastoral ministry since 1978 is the gradual, but radical, transition of ministerial concern from "politicking" to "ministerial competency."[12] It was a historical lesson that the appointment system in Korea made a pastor's concerns vertical (pastor-district superintendent-bishop relation) whereby a pastor's accountability for the parish had been weakened in the past. But after the abolition of the appointment system, pastors had to become more sensitive to the needs of the congregation and to the possibility of upbuilding the community of faith through enrichment of the lay ministry. It might be said that this ministerial change is the prime motif of church growth in Korea.

Another qualitative transformation in Korean Methodism after 1978 is the significant development of the quality of relationships among the pastors and between pastors and district superintendents. If it is not a connectional system in the traditional sense, Korean Methodism is in the process of building its own particular connectionalism based on trust and support. It remains to be seen how effective these connections become.

The third significant outcome is the emergence of so-called "longer pastorates."[13] Bishop Richard B. Wilke affirms the desperate need for longer pastorates by quoting Lyle Schaller, who says that "church growth is strengthened by longer pastorates. Churches with declining memberships often have short-tenured ministries."[14] The longer pastorates that Korean pastors enjoy provide them with greater opportunities to envision long-range ministerial planning and to develop policies related to the upbuilding of the community and the church's mission to the world.

The last significant transformation in Korean Methodism is the affirmation of the people of God through which the laity is becoming an organic part of the total community of faith. The active participation of the laity in every level of the church's life and mission has already contributed to the development of "co-ministry," or team ministry with the pastor.

But in all fairness, it must be noted that there are also negative phenomena already appearing which call for our sharpened analysis and concern. One of the dangers that Korean Methodism has encountered is the possibility of falling into what may be called "local churchism," which is a deviation from what is intended to be a "local congregation-centered structure." Some of the pastors who have been successful in their ministry have a tendency to identify the congregation with the domain of their eternal rule. There has been a grave concern that there will be a shift from longer pastorates to lifelong pastorates. All these dangers may lead the Korean Methodist Church to abandon connectionalism altogether.

A Theological Critique

If Ernst Troeltsch's initial analogy—that is, "church type" and "sect type"—is adopted,[15] Korean Methodism may be interpreted to have been moving from the "church type" to the "sect type." In biblical terms, the church type is symbolized by the "cult of the Ark," whereas the sect type is symbolized by the "cult of the Tent." If the church type or cult of the Ark is structurally institutional and sacramental, the sect type or cult of the Tent in its nature is anti-institutional and rather intimate.

The fact that the Korean Methodist Church abolished the appointment system could indicate that it is moving gradually into the sect type of church. This is surely a concern which confronts the church today and tomorrow. At the same time, the question may be raised about whether the preservation of connectionalism with the guaranteed appointment system (the church type) is the answer to the problems that the churches face; for example, the decline of membership.

Needed here is a reaffirmation of what is stated about John Wesley in The United Methodist Church's *Book of Discipline.* "In the beginning Wesley had thought of his fellows not as constituting a church but simply as forming so many societies."[16] If this means that Wesley had no intention of building another denomination or church separate from the Church of England, Wesley's theology of "many societies" is not to mean a sectarian ecclesiology but an "ecclesiolae in ecclesia,"[17] small, voluntary associations within the larger body of Christians. It is to be understood that the sole purpose of Wesley's movement was to renew the Church of England from below.

The tabernacle model, or synagogue model, or ecclesia of the first church model may be seen as yet a third model combining the previous two. Robert A. Evans designates this model as "communitas" which is "an area of common living" and "a quality of relatedness."[18] The concept of communitas, embracing both the institution and the intimacy, presents itself as an alternative for Korean Methodism to follow.

While the future of Korean Methodism is unpredictable, one thing is certain. The future depends neither on the appointment system, which has proved a failure in Korea, nor on the local churchism or congregationalism, which might lead to an extreme individualism, but on the formation and upbuilding of a "communitas" of faith and service where a "quality of relatedness" may be experienced between God and people, people and people, and the people and the world. I look with expectation to this third model of "ecclesiolae in ecclesia" as the standard for the Korean Methodist Church, and perhaps for fellow Methodists throughout the world as well.

CHAPTER 3

Without Reserve: A Critical Appreciation of the Itineracy

William B. Oden

A historian of Christian ministry has concluded that clergy are "products of a long evolution punctuated by success and failure, forgotten truths and remembered falsehoods, historical accident and (a believer would say), divine plan."[1] It might be argued that United Methodism's heritage of itineracy—its unique system of making clergy appointments—falls into each of those categories.

In this chapter I wish to affirm its success, acknowledge its failures, be reminded of its forgotten truths, confess its falsehoods, note its beginnings as historical accident, and finally, as a believer, suggest that United Methodist itineracy is a part of God's plan of sharing the urgency of the good news of Jesus Christ with all people, and that the itineracy, by being redeemed and renewed, will continue to be essential to the future of The United Methodist Church.

Itineracy and Methodism are so connected that one cannot be spoken of without the other. The primary meaning of itineracy in the *Sixth Oxford Dictionary of Current English* (1978) is "traveling from place to place." Two examples are given: "[of justices] traveling on circuit; [of Methodists] preaching in various circuits." The dictionary then defines *itineracy* (or alternate spelling "itinerancy") as to "be itinerant esp. preach in circuits."

Defenders of Methodist itineracy have argued that the practice is biblically modeled by Jesus' "sending" his disciples out (Matthew 10:5); by the parable of the wedding feast where the servants were to "Go out . . . and invite all you can find" (Matthew 22:9); and by the mission of the seventy sent by Jesus in pairs "like lambs among wolves." These "itinerant" messengers were admonished to go with urgency from town to town, staying in homes, eating where invited, healing the sick, and announcing that "the Kingdom of God has come close to you" (Luke 10:1-9). This sense of urgency to the point of abandoning all else for the sake of the gospel is found in the Great Commission where authority to go into all the world is given by the resurrected Christ to make disciples, baptize, and teach.[2] These are the beginnings of the urgency of itineracy. No advocate of itineracy has claimed that it is biblically *mandated,* only biblically *based.*

Bound in Special Covenant

The 1988 *Book of Discipline* defines an itineracy that began with John Wesley and Francis Asbury. Paragraph 422 states that "Members in full connection with an Annual Conference . . . are *bound in special covenant* with all the ordained ministers of the Annual Conference." The paragraph notes that "they offer themselves without reserve to be appointed and to serve, *after consultation* [a phrase added in 1980; author's italics], as the appointive authority may determine." This "special covenant" is one of "mutual trust and concern."

The word *covenant* has biblical foundations that are familiar to us all. It is used in various ways in Wesleyan tradition, but three are most common. One is the covenant of care and accountability of the early Methodist classes and societies (small disciplined groups of laity under lay leadership). Another is the "Covenant Service," a liturgy written by John Wesley, which uses older Puritan sources, was tied to New Year's watch night and includes the haunting words, "Put me to what thou wilt . . . put me to doing, put me to suffering." Third is the covenant of traveling (itinerant) preachers. This is a covenant that has changed little for 250 years. It began early (1738) in the Methodist revival when three lay preachers came to John Wesley and asked to join him in his itinerant ministry.[3] He later wrote that *they* asked *him* and that he dare not refuse them.[4] Late in 1739, Wesley agreed to meet with his helpers annually in London to fix their business for the year, and also to meet quarterly, as well as to share accounts of their ministry with one another each month. This was the "embryo of the Conference which would begin in 1744."[5]

The key point is that the earliest preachers of Methodism asked Wesley to be allowed to be his assistants. Wesley's authority to appoint his helpers and preachers, and to organize their work, had two sources: the covenant they made with Wesley to go where sent, and the Model Deed of 1763 (followed by the "Deed of Declaration of 1784"), which gave first Wesley, then the Conference, doctrinal foundations and trusteeship of all Methodist property. The implications of this two-pronged authority are most significant. The Deeds gave theological and biblical foundations to the movement, and established ultimate control of the meeting houses and chapels to the Conference, and through the Conference, to the appointed preacher in charge. This process became tempered by lay leadership in later years, but the basic legal structure upon which itineracy was built remains today. Thus Wesley guarded against the "localism" of the sects, which his catholic (universal) side very much opposed. Wesley once said, "As long as I live the people shall have no share in choosing either stewards or leaders among the Methodists. We have not and never had any such custom." [6]

From these very significant beginnings of itineracy, Wesley could send his preachers at a moment's notice to wherever need called. He could say, "the world is my parish," which is an understanding of mission quite different from the sects that (in Wesley's eye) believed that "the parish is my world." [7] While Methodism certainly had some classic marks of a sect (e.g., charismatic leader, conversionist mentality which called the sinner out of the world into a disciplined life of holiness, counterculture dress), Methodism could never be typed. It sought to balance its urgent conversionist mentality with a passion for sacramental spiritual nurture.[8]

Thus the same Wesleyan seeds of itineracy held the kernel of the connection (the early Methodist spelling is "connexion"). The word implies "a chain and a network rather than a merely local cluster of adherents."[9] Charles Wesley's hymn captures this beautifully: "Help us to help each other, Lord, Our little stock improve."

The itinerants had their own covenant with Wesley and each other as well as being a part of the wider covenant (connexion) of Methodism. Their covenant centered upon an agreement to go where sent and through mutual trust and support to uphold one another's ministry.

It is not my assignment to trace the history of itineracy, but it must be said that the seeds of Wesleyan itineracy were sown in America through the ordination and election of Francis Asbury as General Superintendent. And the seeds found fertile soil. Out of the Christmas Conference in 1784, twelve (or thirteen) newly ordained itinerants, along with the attending lay preachers, covenanted together in the Conference "to reform the continent and spread spiritual holiness," submitting themselves to Asbury's appointive power. With passionate urgency, these itinerants carved a new church (some would later say the most representative of America) out of a fast-expanding frontier. While other church communions stayed put with their "localism" tendencies, Methodists "moved" because they believed in moving, in spreading, in seeking, in being in motion, in going from place to place. In a word, they were itinerants because their sense of urgent mission called for an orderly, clearly defined, functional, appointive process. And understanding themselves to be called by God, they covenanted to submit themselves willingly to this process. They offered themselves "without reserve."

The Cost of Missional Urgency

For a Methodist itinerant, to give oneself without reserve in frontier America meant to give not counting the cost, to give at the expense of physical and emotional health, and to give in spite of hardships and obstacles. We have romanticized the itineracy of the circuit riders—and with good reason. Their giving without reserve created American Methodism.

But circuit riders had short life-spans. Even Asbury, with his burning desire to be on the road continually ("I must ride or die"), was often ill and suffered poor health. According to one historian:

> Almost half the preachers who died before 1800 were under thirty years of age at the time of their death, and up to 1844 approximately half died before reaching the age of thirty-three. Of the first 672 preachers whose records were kept in full, two-thirds died before they were to render twelve years of service.[10]

The Methodist Episcopal Church, South, mandated a two-year limit on pastorates when it structured itself in 1844. The one exception was New Orleans, where it took at least two years to build up immunity to yellow fever. It was decided that those who could survive two years should be allowed to continue to serve!

It should be noted also that Asbury's strong (monarchical) episcopacy had dissension from the beginning. This, along with the hardships of itineracy, caused almost one-half of the 1,616 traveling ministers in America (to the year 1814) to locate.[11]

The Loss of Missional Urgency

In less than two centuries we have moved from an Asburyan frontier itineracy (primarily a single and celibate itineracy often compared with monastic movements) to a settled itineracy with parsonages and, more often than not, parsonage families, and to longer pastorates and widening salary ranges for full-time itinerants. We have had a radical shift from the priority of saving souls (converting and discipling new Christians into the flock) and serving the poor to a priority of pastoral care within the flock. According to Dale E. Dunlap: "The simplest description of what has happened to the system of itineracy in American Methodism is that it has undergone a slow but steady change from radical itineracy to localism." The emphasis has moved from itinerant preacher to denominational promoter and parish administrator. True, there have been challenges to the itineracy from the beginning, and bishops have continually admonished the church to return to a missional itineracy (see the Episcopal Addresses of 1844, 1912, and 1988). But the reality is that the face of itineracy has been reshaped dramatically over these 200 plus years. It began on horseback with courageous circuit riders taking vows of *poverty* (a salary of $64 per year), *chastity* (Asbury all but forbade married clergy), and *obedience.* A story steeped in Southern Methodism is told by Lovett H. Weems. It was the tradition for all itinerants to surround the altar rail when appointments were read by the bishop as Annual Conference closed. As each name was called, the itinerant would step forward, hear the appointment for the first time, and reply "God is good. Thank you, Bishop." One brother, not expecting to move, cried out: "Good God, Bishop!"[12]

As the frontier gave way to urbanized industrial America, Methodist preachers got down from horseback, married, moved into parsonages, and became professionals. Ministry has evolved into a multifaceted, highly complex calling-profession with stresses and strains unimaginable to Wesley and Asbury—unimaginable even to contemporary United Methodists who have not struggled with itineracy in its present form.

These stresses and strains are understandable. We do not live in the world of Wesley and Asbury. We are a pluralistic culture made up of a mosaic of subcultures. Seismic shifts have occurred in human consciousness. Old authoritarian patterns have disintegrated in church and society all around the globe. Our ministry is contextualized in living, changing communities. Our structures have not adequately addressed this reality. It is not enough to say, "If only our pastors were more dedicated. . . ." We must respond with creative faithfulness to new "pressure points"[13] on itineracy.

A Parade of Pressure Points

Any "laundry" list of pressure points on the system of itineracy will be general or incomplete. Here is mine:

1. *Two-career families.* Itineracy is more compatible when the spouse has a mobile occupation such as teaching. (Though one could argue that this is not accurate because teaching as a tenured career is difficult for an itinerant's spouse.) It is much more difficult when the spouse is a physician, lawyer, accountant, owner of a business, etc. One spouse said it clearly, "I married a woman who later decided to be an itinerant minister. Where does that leave me?"

2. *Housing allowances instead of parsonages.* The movement of pastors toward owning their own homes is more popular when real estate values are escalating. While parsonages are seen as "perks" by laity, they require sacrifices by clergy and benefit churches more than clergy. But can there be a true itinerant system without a parsonage system?

3. *Limited appointments for women and minorities.* Currently, out of 19,900 United Methodist pastors, 2,776 are women and 2,036 are racial-ethnic pastors. Statistics show that pastors in these categories often serve smaller churches at lower salaries. While The United Methodist Church is officially committed to open itineracy, congregational resistance continues.

4. *New and non-traditional life-styles of pastors.* The number of single clergy is on the upswing, including the number of separated and divorced clergy. This reality forces new imaging of the "parsonage family" in many congregations.

5. *The diverse understandings of consultation.* Laity sometimes see their role as "deciding on" or "calling" their pastors. Pastor-Parish Relations Committees can understand themselves as "pulpit committees" or "search committees." Very often, members of these committees have come from other denominations and have little understanding of the itinerant system. Pastors are more and more frequently letting it be known where they wish to serve as well as turning down appointments.

6. *Self-limiting family concerns.* Healthy environment, the

nearness of medical facilities, and the quality of the school system are often used as reasons for not accepting appointments. As one pastor said, "I will go anywhere in this Annual Conference after my kids are out of school, but before that time, I will not sacrifice their education or safety for the sake of an appointment."[14]

7. *Commitment of pastors to unofficial groups and caucuses.* Pastors are often more difficult to appoint if their commitment to caucuses or unofficial groups within United Methodism gives narrowing focus to their pastoral work. "Is she 'Good News'?" "Will he try to organize a chapter of MFSA or BMCR?" These often become pertinent questions for consideration in the consultative process.

8. *A rigid seniority system.* William Willimon argues that a "clearly recognized and accepted seniority system"[15] has evolved in our itineracy. Often the years of service and salary become the determinate factors in the appointive process. According to Willimon, "When this happens, ministers are sent to churches in which the skills of the pastor are not appropriate to the needs of the congregation. The mission of the church receives less attention than the professional advancement of the minister."[16]

9. *Growing salary disparity.* Clergy compensation in North American United Methodism may be the most complex and threatening of the pressure points on itineracy. Too often salary is the primary consideration in appointment making. Highest salaries are now about five times entry level. Twenty-five years ago, they were two and one-half to three times entry level salaries. The widening salary disparity, according to one pastor, "erodes the meaning of the special covenant into which ordained pastors enter."

10. *Appointments beyond the local church.* Pastors who are appointed beyond the local church in certain categories are often actually "employed" by an agency or institution (in fact, Par. 442, 1988 *Book of Discipline,* uses this exact term) and, because of the guaranteed appointment, must be re-entered into a pastorate at their request.

11. *Large-church pastors.* Studies have shown that pastoral tenure increases with the size of church. Larger congregations produce longer pastorates. Churches of 3,000 or more members keep their pastors much longer—sometimes 10 to 20 years. While there can be positive results of long pastorates, for all practical purposes, these churches are often taken out of itineracy and operate on a "call" system. A "two-tier" appointive track may have come into being with different rules and processes for each tier. There are tenure

limits for bishops serving in one area and tenure limits for General Secretaries of Boards and Agencies. District superintendents are limited to six years. Some argue that there should be a tenure limit restored for pastors. Others suggest that would create more problems than it would solve.

As one considers this parade of pressure points on itineracy, the question must be asked: Is this phrase "without reserve" still operational? For over 200 years, "without reserve" stood by itself, both implicitly and explicitly in our *Discipline.* But the words became weighted down. After several attempts (beginning with the Uniting Conference of 1939), additional words were voted by the 1980 General Conference: "without reserve . . . after consultation." This significant change affirmed that itineracy is a three-way connection: bishop and cabinet, pastor, and laity in the local churches to which the appointment is being made. But there are few guidelines for consultation, and each bishop and cabinet determines policy and practice of the consultative process.[17]

Taking the pressure points into account, one could argue that "without reserve" has lost much of its meaning. New circumstances, conflicting covenants, fast-changing social order, vows that may have lost meaning, words stripped of will and resolve, all combine to prompt a central question: Is today's "settled itineracy" another name for the "localism" that Methodists have feared from the beginning? And if so, can a settled itineracy be transformed into a revitalized strategy for mission which also takes seriously issues of justice, equity, and a renewed sense of urgency to spread scriptural holiness?

Redeeming and Renewing the Itineracy

It is out of this matrix of concerns, tensions, and questions that the Council of Bishops called upon The United Methodist Church in the 1988 Episcopal Address to "redeem and renew the itineracy." At the same time a Commission for the Study of Ministry reported to General Conference that issues of injustice and inequity, as well as accountability, availability, and authority, must be addressed in the appointive process if the itineracy is to remain a viable option for the church. But I fear that too great a load has been placed on the itineracy as the key to restoring Wesleyan vitality. Other communions face many of the same problems in relation to their clergy. Edward Schillebeeckx wrote on issues of ministry from the Roman Catholic perspective,[18] reflecting on the Catholic bishops' attempt to address the problems and issues surrounding representative ministry in Catholicism. While Schillebeeckx acknowledges that "the future of church communities and ministry within them is determined not only by the community of the church but also the churches' leadership,"[19] he also calls attention to a passionate speech made by Bishop Bellido of Peru in the Catholic bishops' debate on ministry: "Any attempt at changing an infrastructure [in this case the priesthood] within a greater structure [the church] without changing the greater structure is a Utopia."[20]

The bishop's point applies equally to United Methodism. Itineracy cannot be redeemed and renewed apart from a redeemed and renewed sense of mission; apart from a redeemed and renewed clergy and laity; apart from a redeemed and renewed episcopacy.

Why retain itineracy? Opinions range from "If it's not broke, why fix it?" to "It's broke and can't be fixed." The basic, and perhaps only, legitimate question to ask of itineracy is this: Is it still an effective missional strategy for deploying pastors? Dennis Campbell points out that Wesley's ideas about itineracy were articulated and applied by Asbury to the American church; that while there were periodic challenges, "The dominant sentiment was that God's will was working in the church, and that the appointive system, with an itinerant ministry, was an effective means of ordering ministry for the urgent evangelical task." This urgent task was grounded in the preachers' conviction that their work was "part of a grand plan which had ultimate significance. The deprivations and difficulties of the earthly life paled in comparison with the hopes and promises of the church triumphant."[21] These are heady words and strong convictions. There is no doubt that creeping localism (the parish is my world), loss of the sense of urgency in the evangelistic task, even secularism with its loss of transcendence, have all weakened the radical itineracy of the past.

Yet, we parallel frontier society in significant ways. Just as the westward frontier movement fragmented a stable society, creating a transitional one, so also our own social structures are fast changing: growing individualism, radical changes in our basic institutions of family and government, shifting populations, and a high-tech information-oriented communication system are all indications of such changes.

Itineracy can be most effective in transitional times. In such times, a highly mobile, quickly deployed, accountable, well-resourced and supervised ministry is (almost by definition) a missional ministry. But definition of our mission as a church is precisely the problem: is it not still the biblical mandate to make disciples, baptize, teach, nurture, and lead a congregation to share in this same ministry?[22] If its mission is primarily to provide pastoral care to an existing flock and little else, then itineracy becomes only a way to rearrange pastors and churches.

Itineracy As Missional Strategy

As a *missional strategy,* the connectional itineracy of The United Methodist Church is a valid and faithful expression of fulfilling the Great Commission. It is a *living* tradition that is capable of serving the church as productively in the future as it has in the past.

Frankly, the issue before The United Methodist Church is not an itinerant vs. nonitinerant ministry. The issue is that of a *vital itineracy* that is *"redeemed and renewed"* or a *weakened itineracy that reacts defensively to all the pressure points on the system*—for no other system of ministerial deployment is more faithful or effective within the United Methodist theological framework.[23] The connection is an organic body of accountability and love for the sake of mission. God calls us to our common mission and "places" us in the connection. Those called to representative ministry are "bound in special covenant" and appointed as itinerants to a covenant within a covenant. The linchpin of itineracy as missional strategy is the affirmation that in spite of all the pressures and polarities surrounding appointment making, those who have covenanted together in the traveling ministry do so trusting "that God's will is worked out in the appointment process."

The "call" system may be as appropriate to nonconnected individual congregations as the itineracy is to United Methodism. But even when objectively analyzed, the call system is no panacea. *The Christian Century* recently reported on a "halfway house" for fired clergy. The article pointed out that because of theological polarization in congregations of a sister denomination, there was little security, and in fact, "any Baptist minister can find himself thrown out on his ear for almost anything."[24] It further noted: "A 1988 study conducted by the Southern Baptist Sunday School Board in Nashville found that more than 2,100 Southern Baptist pastors were fired during an 18-month period, a 31 percent increase over the figure in a similar survey conducted in 1984."

A committee that uses the call system in seeking a pastor will often mirror its own theology, values, and style of leadership. This can cause the criteria of pastoral needs to be reduced to a common denominator of the committee's combined experiences. As one "call system" pastor said recently, "It cuts the prophetic nerve from my ministry to look out over the congregation and preach to the very ones who totally control my continuance!" Note also that many bishops frequently have pastors seeking admission into The United Methodist Church from denominations that are using the call system.

The presbyterial system, which several communions employ, also has its strengths and weaknesses. The system uses a "negotiated" pastoral call in which a number of "rules of procedure" are followed by both a regional committee and a local church committee. Using a detailed and lengthy process (often taking at least a year), a contract/covenant is arrived at which is agreeable to the local church, the called pastor, and the regional denominational body. Usually this system produces longer pastorates. (In English Methodism, the invitation is for five years with extensions of up to three more. It is possible to curtail the appointment if things are not going well.)

In the Presbyterian Church, U.S.A., the covenant/contract is permanent and cannot be broken by one party without the consent of the other two. This can mean a pastor who has no other place to go might stay in a church long past the point of effectiveness. While some elements of the presbyterial approach have been incorporated into The United Methodist Church through consultation, there is still a major difference between consulting and negotiating. Though some would argue that this is true more in theory than practice, the difference is significant. In negotiating, any one party can veto the process. In the United Methodist itinerant system, after consultation, the bishop appoints.

The itinerant system of deployment of clergy grew out of a passionate desire to share the gospel, to save souls, to go where the people are—*all people,* not just one class or segment of society. Itineracy is sending pastors, quickly and efficiently, to a place of service. This model of deployment carries a significant perspective to the local church. In the call system and the presbyterial system, the local church's self-professed needs become the decisive factor. In the itinerant system, these are taken into account but there is (or should be) the global vision and evangelistic urgency that the bishop and cabinet bring to an appointment. The itinerant system of deploying pastors has the history and contemporary possibility of a bishop-cabinet/laity/pastor partnership that binds the mission of United Methodism to the mission of the local church. Clergy move so they can move the congregations into witness and service in the community and the world. Itinerant pastors exist not just to provide pastoral care but to develop itinerant congregations who view the world as their parish.

While the itinerant system may have been born out of Wesley's pragmatic need to respond quickly to a fast-expanding revival, it also has a theological foundation that is Wesleyan to the core. Itineracy is the Wesleyan doctrine of sanctification translated into polity. It calls for the total yielding of the self to the Spirit through a covenant of care and accountability.

A Connectional Church Necessitates an Itinerant Ministry

I see no viable alternative to the itinerant ministry for The United Methodist Church as long as we are a connectional church committed to reforming our lands and spreading scriptural holiness. This does not discount the "pressure points" upon itineracy. But those very points are often where the missional urgency of the good news rubs raw against the direction of our culture. And as the church seeks to redeem and renew the itineracy, these pressure points cannot always be smoothed over. The scandal of the good news is ever present in the church's missional strategy.

What other missional strategy would more ably match congregational needs with a pastor's gift and grace, providing every church a pastor and every pastor a church? The system does not always make good matches. Neither does any other system of deployment. But with consultation that includes supportive evaluation between pastor and Pastor-Parish Relations Committee (Par. 423), with supportive supervision by the district superintendent (Par. 520.2), an orderly pastoral change can occur.

What other missional strategy would better actualize the faithful placement of women, clergy couples, and racial-ethnic pastors in our churches, and would be an advocate for cross-racial and cross-cultural pastorates? While progress has been slow, there has been progress! If left to the vote (or veto power) of local churches, the diversity of color, culture, and gender in our pulpits would be severely limited. Because of the appointive system, barriers have fallen and the church is more inclusive.

What other missional strategy would more fully affirm the freedom of the pulpit by not allowing it to become a temperature gauge of popularity? A prophetic preacher said of Bishop G. Bromley Oxnam, who had saved the pastor from being forced out of his pulpit, "He demonstrated the genius of the . . . Methodist system of appointments, for it is the greatest invention for the support of freedom in the pulpit the Christian movement has ever seen."[25]

What other missional strategy would be better suited to supply the poor and oppressed with the glad tidings of salvation? Bishop McKendree first related itineracy to the beginning words of Jesus' ministry found in Luke 4:18. Almost two centuries after McKendree, bishops and cabinets send pastors to the inner city and rural poverty areas in a variety of ministries.

What other missional strategy would provide a congregation with a variety of leadership gifts over a long period of time? Pastors have a variety of gifts—preaching, administration, teaching, pastoral care. But seldom does one pastor have all gifts of ministry. Itineracy gives a greater likelihood of "wholeness" in representative ministry. A lay woman recently witnessed, "I've been a Methodist for seventy-two years. I've been hurt, sad, angry, and relieved when my pastors have moved. I can name all fourteen who have served this church since I joined. All have had an impact on me and helped me grow. One I've lost track of. Eight I know are still alive. I pray for each one daily." That is vintage Methodism!

What other missional strategy would respond quickly to the need for the establishment of new congregations and the transformation of declining ones? In other systems, congregations are often left to their own initiatives and resources. Itineracy offers an overall design for church extension and transformation, *but only if fueled by the urgency of the gospel!*

How to Redeem and Renew Itineracy

So how do we begin redeeming and renewing itineracy? Obviously, this is a continuing process as the church struggles with the nature of ministry, ordination, and the appointive process. Laity are now actively involved in the dialogue and are welcome partners, for the *cleros* is within the *laos.* As the itineracy is focused upon and reaffirmed, the time has also come to affirm the place of nonitinerant ministries in The United Methodist Church. Local (lay) pastors and half-itinerants have been a significant part of the missional strategy of Methodism from the beginning. With about one-half of our 38,000 churches having memberships of 100 or less, a new generation of tentmaker lay preachers or nonitinerating ordained pastors is being seriously considered.

Many of the ingredients to redeem and renew the itineracy are already in place or can be put into place by bishops, cabinets, and Boards of Ordained and Diaconal Ministry. These include:

1. *A clear and consistent consultation policy and process.* Pastor-Parish Relations Committee, pastors, and cabinets all need to clarify how consultation relates to each partner. In reality, consultation is not negotiation. We have only begun to flesh out the disciplinary paragraphs related to this area.

2. *The significance of the supervisory role of district superintendents.* When superintendents see ongoing evaluation and supervision of the pastors as an essential and continual element of their job, there will be fewer surprises in the appointive process.

3. *A cabinet environment where confidentiality is lived out in covenant relationship.* Hostility and conflict often exist in the appointive process, and cabinet environment sets the tone for resolution and reconciliation.

4. *A safety net to discover and nurture the overlooked and underutilized.* This is the responsibility of the bishop and cabinet, and is increasingly the beginning focus of appointment making.

5. *A coordinated and consistent process of interpreting the nature of itinerant ministry.* This should begin with candidacy, continue through seminary, and on into the preparation for ordination and conference membership. The meaning of "without reserve" should be clarified early in the process. It is important to include spouses so that groundwork can be laid for dealing with potentially conflicting covenants.

6. *A clarifying and reclaiming process for incompetent and ineffective pastors with track records of destructive patterns toward themselves and/or their congregations.* This is one of the toughest ingredients of a redeemed and renewed itineracy. But it is essential! Pilot programs are beginning to emerge in a number of Annual Conferences.

7. *Exiting procedures that are fair and caring.* Itineracy is not for all who are called to representative ministry. Other expressions of ministry in the church and in the world are just as valid. Testing, counseling, and support should be available to those considering location or a vocational change.

A redeemed and renewed itineracy will not just happen. It will be shaped by strong leadership from the Council of Bishops, the Division of Ordained Ministry, Conference Cabinets, and Boards of Ordained and Diaconal Ministry, and it must include meaningful lay involvement at every level.

The words "without reserve" have been encumbered with a myriad of qualifications. They have been tarnished and are in constant tension with our society. They go against the stream of our cultural values. They are communal and covenantal, not individualistic and privatistic. They depend on mutual trust and accountability, on submission to authority in a permissive age. As Bishop Earl G. Hunt has said, "The whole United Methodist system of deploying ministry seems to be opposed to the basic anti-authoritarian mood of our day."[26]

The truth is there are always reservations in any appointment. But with consultation, they are addressed.[27] In prayerful dialogue with other covenants to which one is bound, the reservations are prioritized. In fear and trembling, the self is then offered in surrender, and an appointment is confirmed.

The words "without reserve" demand sacrifice, discipline, and willingness to submerge one's own ambitions and preferences into a wider vision of the church's needs. They are totally dependent upon a firm commitment to Jesus Christ, the clear call to be God's representative minister, and loyalty to a system that sends where one may not choose to go.

And that call is to GO! Spread the good news of Jesus Christ. How can we spread good news without scattering? How will we scatter unless we are appointed to diverse places? How can we be appointed unless we are willing to go "without reserve"?

CHAPTER 4

Spiritual Discernment in Consultation

M. Kent Millard

The largest church in the conference was open for a new senior pastor. The local church staff-parish committee had met with the district superintendent to develop a profile of the church and to suggest the gifts and graces needed for future pastoral leadership. The total cabinet was meeting to make a decision about who should be appointed as the next senior pastor. In the ensuing discussion, three potential candidates for the position emerged. Each potential senior pastor had advocates within the cabinet who were sure that this pastor was the one with the special gifts needed to minister effectively in the parish under discussion. After about an hour and a half of vigorous debate, it was clear there was no consensus among the cabinet, and the district superintendents were equally divided among the three candidates.

Then the bishop made an unusual recommendation. He recommended a half-hour break and asked each member of the cabinet to go somewhere to be alone and silent and try to listen for the "still, small voice" of God for guidance in this important decision. The recommendation was followed, and a half hour later all the cabinet members returned from their time of solitude. The bishop handed out slips of paper and, without any more discussion, asked each superintendent to write the name of the pastor they felt led to appoint to this parish. The papers were collected, and, to the amazement of all, the decision was nearly unanimous for one particular pastor. The pastor was approached and the church consulted. Once appointed, the person served very effectively for many years.

Without naming it as such, the bishop practiced a process called spiritual discernment in making this appointment. He encouraged the gathering of all the relevant data about the needs of that particular parish and allowed the discussion of the perceived gifts and graces of each of the potential pastors. Then he gave each member of the cabinet some time in solitude to ponder, meditate, and listen for guidance from the Lord. Finally, a decision was made which was not declared to be the absolute will of God, but affirmed as the decision as close to the will of God as that particular cabinet could come, given their own gifts and limitations.

Unfortunately, all too often in the United Methodist system, appointments seem to be made on the basis of the will of the bishop or the will of the district superintendents, or the desire of the church for a particular pastor. Everyone seems to be consulted except God. While acknowledging that all of these other consultations must take place, it is the thesis of this chapter that the process of spiritual discernment provides a way for helping cabinets, pastors, and local churches discern and listen for God's voice in the appointment of pastors in the itinerant system.

The Theology of Spiritual Discernment

The theological premise underlying the practice of spiritual discernment is the doctrine of the omnipresence of God. It is the belief that God is always and everywhere present in the world God has created. The psalmist expresses the doctrine of the omnipresence of God with a sense of wonder and awe:

> Where can I go from your spirit?
> Or where can I flee from your presence?
> If I ascend to heaven, you are there;
> if I make my bed in Sheol, you are there.
> If I take the wings of the morning
> and settle at the farthest limits of the sea,
> even there your hand shall lead me,
> and your right hand shall hold me fast.
> (Ps. 139:7-10)

In John's Gospel, when a Samaritan woman asked Jesus whether God was to be located on Mount Gerizim where the Samaritans had their temple, or in Jerusalem where the Jews had their temple, Jesus responded by assuring her that God is not limited to one physical place: "God is spirit, and those who worship him must worship in spirit and truth" (John 4:24). As the fundamental spiritual reality of life, God is always and everywhere present. Furthermore, in his last words to his disciples, the risen Christ assures his followers of his omnipresence when he says: "All authority in heaven and on earth has been given to me. . . . And remember, I am with you always, to the end of the age" (Matthew 28:18-20). For Christians, God in the form of the risen Christ is always and everywhere present and seeking to provide guidance in our personal and corporate lives.

A theology of spiritual discernment affirms not only God's presence in every moment of life, but also that God is continually seeking to make his will known to those who will listen. In the Lord's Prayer, Jesus taught us to pray, "Your will be done, on earth as it is in heaven" (Matthew 6:10). At the end of the Sermon on the Mount, Jesus said, "Not everyone who says to me, 'Lord, Lord,' will enter the kingdom of heaven, but only the one who *does* the will of my Father in heaven" (Matthew 7:21). And Jesus himself, when he came to the final hours of his earthly life, prayed in the Mount of Olives: "Father, if you are willing, remove this cup from me; yet, not my will but yours be done" (Luke 22:42). In these and in many other ways Jesus made it clear that God's will can be both known and followed.

However, since we are fallible human creatures, it is seldom possible for us to see God's will with complete clarity. More often than not, we simply get glimpses or nudges hinting at what the will of God may be in a particular circumstance, and as we take the leap of faith we discover what seems to have been the desire of God. As Paul writes: "For now we see in a mirror, dimly, but then we will see face to face. Now I know only in part; then I will know fully, even as I have been fully known" (I Corinthians 13:12). Nonetheless, it is better to see the will of God in a mirror even dimly than not to get a glimpse of it at all. It is better to know only in part than not to know at all.

To take Paul's analogy a step further, if one wants to see in a mirror, even dimly, one at least has to be in front of the mirror. In other words, the one thing we can do to catch a glimpse of the will of God is to put ourselves in the position where we can apprehend and be apprehended by God. Christians throughout the ages have discovered that the position in which we are most likely to be apprehended by God involves the disciplines of prayer, meditation, scripture reading, silence, and group or individual spiritual guidance. The consistent and intentional practice of these classical spiritual disciplines places us in the context in which a living and vital relationship with God can be established and maintained, and through which glimpses of the will of God can be seen.

Consequently, since we are surrounded by a God who wants us to know and do God's will, the problem is not with God's availability to us, but in our availability to God. God is constantly seeking us in Christ, but we are often so preoccupied with our own desires, schedules, and goals that we have no time or space to practice the disciplines which may make possible a divine encounter. Therefore, we often do not listen for God's guidance on either personal matters or on corporate decisions related to the appointment of pastors in the itinerant system.

The crisis faced in some parts of The United Methodist Church over appointments and the whole itinerant system is basically a crisis of contemplation. Are we convinced that bishops, cabinets, pastors, and churches are committed to practicing the spiritual disciplines so that they may get a glimpse of God's will in the making of appointments?

At a recent workshop on preaching for about seventy-five pastors and seminarians, the leader suggested that before a person could prepare a sermon he or she had to prepare the preacher. The preacher is prepared by the vitality of her or his own living relationship with God, and this relationship is fed and nurtured by the individual's own devotional life. The leader asked the participants to gather in small groups of three or four persons, and to share with each other their own devotional patterns and the resources they found most helpful in their personal prayer life. About 50 percent of the pastors and seminarians present reported they had no pattern of private devotional life, and rarely spent time in personal prayer because they were just too busy with all the demands of parish and seminary life. When one pastor was asked if he *ever* prayed, he responded: "Yes, I offer a pastoral prayer every Sunday in our worship service." Another pastor said he did have a devotional time when he was a layperson before he went into the ordained ministry, but felt he "outgrew that sort of thing in seminary." It is no wonder that there is a crisis in The United Methodist Church with regard to the itineracy, as well as other issues, if a significant number of pastors, and perhaps even some of the bishops and cabinets, have become so involved with the business of the church that they take no time for listening for guidance from the Lord of the church.

The goal of spiritual discernment, as it relates to the itineracy, is to help the leaders of the church at all levels to focus their attention on seeking God's will for the church, rather than seeking to manipulate the system to produce the preconceived results that one group or faction in the church desires. Spiritual discernment refers to the ability to distinguish or to see the difference between the will of God and my own will, or the will of other persons who seek to dominate the itinerant system. Spiritual discernment as a theological process encourages all parts of the itinerant system (bishops, cabinets, pastors, congregations) to practice the spiritual disciplines that develop friendship with God and place one in the setting in which one can catch a glimpse of the will of God in the appointment of pastors.

John Wesley's Pattern for Spiritual Discernment

Even a cursory reading of the life of John Wesley reveals a man who is intensely devoted to personal spiritual disciplines as a way to maintain a living relationship with God.

> To know Wesley is also to know a person of intense and meaningful discipline . . . he gave himself daily to the spiritual disciplines of prayer, Bible study, and devotion. But Discipline was never an end in itself. It was the means to a vital relationship with God and the resulting power that comes from that relationship.[1]

John Wesley placed himself in a context where he saw glimpses of the will of God for himself, and for the budding Methodist movement and its unique system of itinerant pastors.

The foundation of Wesley's devotional patterns was a lifetime discipline of rising early in the morning for a time of prayer, meditation, and study. Wesley normally went to bed by 10:00 P.M. and got up at 4:30 or 5:00 A.M. so that he could spend at least two hours praying, studying the Bible, and reading the classics of devotional literature. John Wesley's life, ministry, and decisions about the itineracy were undoubtedly shaped and influenced by these devotional patterns and his deep desire to find and do the will of God for himself and for the church which grew out of his ministry.

Wesley wrote to one of the itinerant preachers words that still apply to all those who seek to discern the will of God in the midst of the itinerant ministry: "O begin! Fix some part of every day for private exercises. . . . Whether you like it or not, read and pray daily. It is for your life; there is no other way; else you will be a trifler all your days."[2] Unfortunately, significant numbers of Wesley's followers have failed to fix some part of every day for private exercises and have indeed become "triflers" in the church.

While John Wesley models and recommends an exemplary pattern of personal devotion, he also reveals an attitude of authoritarianism in his appointment of pastors. Wesley began the itinerant system for the placement of pastors in an era when the "divine right of kings" was assumed, and the pastors and congregations under his leadership were mainly uneducated and new to the Christian faith. In those historical circumstances, Wesley felt that it was incumbent upon him to discern the will of God alone, without consultation from the pastor or societies involved.

John Wesley laid down certain unalterable conditions for itinerant preachers which are articulated in "The Large Minutes." In question twenty-seven he is asked, "What power is this which you exercise over both the preachers and the societies?" In his answer he refers to the first itinerating preachers and concludes that they are:

> To serve me as sons, and to labor when and where I should direct . . . and here commenced my power, to appoint each of these when, and where, and how to labour . . . the case continued the same when the number of preachers increased. I had just the same power still to appoint when, and where and how each should help me.[3]

Wesley had the power to appoint, and he apparently made all the decisions himself without consulting with other elders, pastors, or the society involved. When pastors or societies asked about the possibility of a preacher staying in the same society for at least a year, he replied: "I know, were I myself to preach one whole year in one place, I should preach both myself and most of my congregation asleep. . . . We have found by a long and constant experience that a frequent change of preachers is best."[4]

Wesley's ideal was that preachers would travel around a circuit, staying with each society no longer than two weeks and then change to a new circuit every year. The positive result of this system was the establishment of Methodist societies all over England and the United States. The negative result was the cost in human effort and sacrifice for the itinerating preachers, with many dying young or being worn out before they were forty. The miracle that such a demanding system worked at all is testimony to the deep respect preachers and societies had for Wesley's walk with God, and to their own lives of personal devotion and commitment.

When Methodism came to the United States, Francis Asbury served the same role in America that John Wesley served in England. Asbury also appointed preachers without the consultation of others. Both Wesley and Asbury were eager to do the will of God in leading the church, but apparently believed that God's will could best be discerned by acting alone in the placement of pastors in their particular historical situations.

However, after Wesley and Asbury passed from the scene, their successors felt the need for consultation with other elders in seeking God's will for the placement of pastors. William McKendree was elected bishop in 1801 and became Asbury's successor. McKendree introduced the practice of consulting with the cabinet on ministerial appointments and got around Asbury's objection to this innovation by explaining that "unlike his old father in the faith, he needed the help of presiding elders."[5] Thus from the very early days the leaders after Wesley and Asbury felt the need to consult with other elders on the cabinet in order to catch a glimpse of the will of God in appointment making. This process of broadening the scope of consultation has continued up to contemporary times with the inclusion of input from the cabinet, the pastors, and the congregations involved.

The goal of Wesley and Asbury was to live in such close relationship with God through their daily discipline that they could discern God's will for the placement of pastors. Their successors have also discovered that a living and vital relationship to God is necessary in leading the church. But they have also discovered that God may speak through pastors and congregations, and therefore consultations with those parties is essential for the contemporary discernment of God's will for the placement of pastors.

If the itinerant system for the placement of pastors is to be an effective instrument for God in our time, those who administer the system (bishops, cabinets, pastors, and local church leaders) need to recover the personal and corporate disciplines out of which the itinerant system first grew and developed. This does not mean that the itinerant system will be practiced in the twentieth century in the same way it was practiced in the eighteenth century. Since it is a constantly evolving system, the fervent desire to do the will of God which characterized the founder of the itinerant system can still be the chief motivating force for the twentieth-century leaders of this system.

Spiritual Discernment and Contemporary Itineracy

The goal of the itinerant system should be to seek the will of God in the placement of pastors. In discerning God's will over the course of time, The United Methodist Church has been led to the importance of consultation. Because of the increasing complexity of congregations with unique needs, and ministries and pastors with special gifts and family situations, it is not possible for one person acting alone to adequately discern God's will in any given situation. God reveals a portion of his will to each party in the appointment process (bishop, cabinet, pastor, congregation) and each needs the other in order to "see in a mirror dimly" what God may be desiring.

Consultation in appointment making is defined by The United Methodist Church in this way:

> Consultation is the process whereby the bishop and/or district superintendent confer with the pastor and Committee on Pastor-Parish Relations, taking into consideration the criteria of paragraph 532, a performance evaluation, needs of the appointment under consideration, and mission of the church.[6]

Ideally, this consultation is not simply to ask the pastor what he or she wants or to ask the pastor-parish relations committee what they want.

When spiritual discernment is the model for making appointments, the pastor and congregation are asked what they perceive to be the will of God for them at this time in their lives and ministry. Because of the nature of sin and our tendency to seek our own will, this is not the kind of question that can be answered quickly or easily. God often does not give the answer to this question hastily but usually requires adequate time for brooding, pondering, praying, and listening. With our contemporary desire for quick solutions, it is hard for us to "wait upon the Lord" for the guidance we need. However, the alternative is simply for us to push a decision through, that often is the decision of the most powerful or influential party in the appointment system rather than a decision that reflects the spirit and will of God.

The process used in making appointments is as important as the appointment itself. An appointment-making process that does not reflect the spirit and mind of Christ can never produce a result reflecting the life and ministry of our risen Savior. In order to reflect the spirit of Christ in appointment making, cabinets may need to spend much more time with pastors and parishes (and less in conference meetings!), so that decisions made reflect a broad base of input as well as compassion for those affected by the decisions. Therefore, if bishops and cabinets are to reflect more clearly the mind of Christ in making appointments, they need to take very seriously the light of divine insight that comes through the prayers of the pastor and parish involved.

In applying the principles of spiritual discernment to the contemporary situation, a district superintendent and pastor might well spend time praying for each other before meeting together to discuss the pastor's future appointment, and share prayer together when they meet to make it clear that their goal is to seek the will of God. When the district superintendent consults with the staff parish relations committee, she or he needs to lead that committee in times of prayer and meditation as they all seek to open themselves to guidance from God. When the bishop and cabinet meet they need to constantly remind themselves that Christ is head of the church and their task is to allow Christ to exert leadership through their decisions.

Danny Morris suggests a model for spiritual discernment in which the question under discussion is imagined to be at the center of the group as a diamond.[7] At every meeting between district superintendent and pastor, at every meeting of district superintendent, pastor and parish, and at every cabinet meeting, the question of which pastor should be appointed to a specific church ought to be seen as a multifaceted diamond that reflects its light to each person in the group somewhat differently. Each person then shares the light he or she sees, realizing that it is not the total spectrum, but it is one ray of light that has been revealed. The process is continued until the light from the diamond itself presents the answer and those observing have a strong sense of the leading of God.

Our Quaker brothers and sisters have used this kind of group discernment process for many years and have been led in remarkable ways by God. However, they have discovered that such a process takes a great deal more time to arrive at a sense of clarity within the group. Douglas V. Steere says that there is an old Quaker rule that says, "When in doubt, wait."[8] Having served on the cabinet under the pressure of a rapidly approaching Annual Conference, I can affirm that sometimes it appears that the United Methodist rule is "when in doubt, appoint."

While the United Methodist *Discipline* empowers the bishop and cabinet to make appointments at any time of year, the assumption is that most appointments will be made at each Annual Conference session. This assumption sometimes causes decisions to be made in haste without giving adequate time for listening for the "still, small voice" of God. Appointments should be made and fixed when the cabinet, pastor, and congregation have a clear sense of the leading of God, which may or may not be in the spring of each year. Congregations may need to be vacant for a few weeks or even months while they are in the process of discernment with the cabinet on who God may be calling to serve a particular parish. Pastors may also need to learn to wait patiently while sharing the light they see regarding their next appointment. In a compulsive society driven to move at a faster and faster pace, the call to "wait upon the Lord" will sound strange indeed. However, perhaps the church can provide a new model for faithful living that relies more on listening with the ears than on running with the feet.

God has used the itinerant system for the placement of pastors in a marvelous way to lead people to Christ and to serve the missional needs of the world. It has been the system that characterized Methodism throughout the world for more than 250 years. However, the system has evolved over the years from one person's consultation with God, to a cabinet's consultation with God, to a consultation with God which is shared by cabinet, pastor, and parish alike. This evolving itinerant system finds its core and functions most effectively when all those who are a part of it (bishops, cabinets, pastors, and congregations) focus on seeking and doing the will of God and live personal lives of obedience to God.

Loyalty to the founder of Methodism is not found in a rigid repetition of his methods of appointment making, but in developing a similar deep desire to live in a vital relationship with God, out of which God can lead us in our time. The itinerant system and the people who live and work in it will find renewed vitality when spiritual discernment becomes once again the primary focus.

CHAPTER 5

Reaffirming the Covenant in Itineracy

Donald H. Treese

The itinerant system is the accepted method of The United Methodist Church by which ordained ministers are appointed by bishops to fields of labor. All ordained ministers shall accept and abide by these appointments. (Par. 437)

Through appointment making the connectional nature of the United Methodist system is made visible. (Par. 530.1)

. . . There are stresses that must be addressed if the connectional principle is to continue to serve us well in the future. . . . Stresses include issues surrounding clergy itineracy and the appointment process. (Par. 112.4)

The Book of Discipline, 1988

The Episcopal Address to the 1988 General Conference outlined the direction United Methodism is headed as the twenty-first century approaches. Immediately preceding a strong affirmation that we are going to be a growing church going on to perfection, and immediately following a similar affirmation that we are going to be a more evangelical, socially responsible, singing, inclusive, global, and connectional church came the assertion that "we are going to redeem and renew the itineracy."[1]

The "redemption and renewal" of the itineracy is a chord that has been struck explicitly and implicitly over the long history of episcopal addresses. In 1844 the address dealt with debilitating influences upon the energies of the itinerant system, focusing on the enervating practice of young preachers to marry before joining the itinerant system.[2] In John Wesley's writing about itineracy there is a thread of lament and frustration over why so many of his "helpers" resented and resisted the system of itineracy: "They can give me 20 reasons for going elsewhere!"[3]

These references reflect the continuous interaction of the itinerant system with the connectional principle of Methodism and its mission in the world. It is a system in which all United Methodists participate as thousands of pastoral appointments are made each year, following the consultation with pastors and lay representatives of the local churches involved. So crucial is this interaction that in 1988 the General Conference implied that the future of connectionalism required a healthy system of itineracy: "There are stresses that must be addressed if the connectional principle is to continue to serve as well in the future. The stresses include issues surrounding clergy itineracy and the appointment process."[4]

This chapter seeks to address some of the issues urgently facing itineracy that must be more carefully considered and more responsibly handled if the stresses noted above are to be alleviated.

Itineracy and Covenant

If itineracy is to be "redeemed and renewed," it cannot be done apart from the clergy covenant of the annual conference. The "covenant paragraph" in *The Book of Discipline* is all too seldom consulted when addressing ordained ministry issues in general and itineracy in particular. This paragraph speaks of the special relationship among ordained ministers which they, by virtue of election and ordination, promise to keep in various ways, including offering "themselves without reserve to be appointed, and to serve, after consultation, as the appointive authority may determine." They live with their sisters and brothers "in mutual trust and concern and seek with them the sanctification of the fellowship."[5]

The commitment called for in this covenant is a radical one. Giving up control of one's vocational life is an expression of radical obedience to God and the church. To be chosen and to agree to a servant mode of ministry—to be "under orders"—is a rare counter-culture act in the final decade of the twentieth century. Ultimately, it means living out the consequences of this radical choice with a "holy indifference" to the outcome. But it need not be lived out in isolation; it should be lived out in a caring, supportive covenant relationship sometimes referred to as "the congregation of the clergy."

The fact that this is foreign language to many clergy and laity today is perhaps the most urgent issue facing itineracy. It is not unusual to find itineracy and covenant celebrated more by those who transfer into an Annual Conference from congregational systems than by those who have always served within it. The power and promise behind the language are not being clearly articulated for women and men as they prepare to enter the covenant and the itinerant system. Without this articulation, conference membership and ordination can cynically be viewed as similar to the "hoops" required for initiation and membership into secular organizations and systems.

Bishops, boards of ordained ministry, and related leadership must move quickly and dramatically to become interpreters of itineracy. On at least four occasions in a candidate's preparation there is good opportunity for clear articulation of the expectations and obligations of the itinerant system: (1) When candidates are exploring their call to ordained ministry, pastors and pastor-parish relations committees should take the initiative in discussing this accepted method by which ordained ministers are appointed in The United Methodist Church. (2) *The Book of Discipline* requires that the district committee on ordained ministry receive from all candidates written evidence that they understand the expectations and obligations of itineracy. (3) Boards of ordained ministry are charged with a similar duty toward candidates for probationary membership, associate membership, and full connection. In fact, at the time of examination for full connection the candidates are to reflect on how the actual practice of their ministry has affected their understanding of the itinerant system. (4) In the preparation of ordinands, bishops have a rare and solemn opportunity to engage the newest of the deacons and elders in understanding the covenantal foundation of ordained ministry and the itineracy through which it serves.

In an extended series of conversations across the church with a representative group of bishops, district superintendents, and pastors affirmation was given to the incredible power the covenant relationship continues to hold. However, if leadership neglects the required continuous interpretation, this crucial covenant relationship will inevitably erode. Bishops must reclaim their historic responsibility as interpreters of itineracy. Bishop Nolan B. Harmon once wrote: "Methodist episcopacy in the mind of Asbury was not an end in itself but an instrument to reach a great end, namely, to establish itineracy."[6] In the 1990s the task is effective interpretation. The writings of John Wesley reflect the necessity for constant teaching and interpretation in order to maintain the itineracy as a living expression of a living reality among the clergy. It is tragic for leadership to allow the press of other work to force out its teaching responsibilities.

Without exception, my conversation contacts affirmed that a renewal of the covenant relationship could prevent and solve many of the problems in itinerant ministry.

Itineracy and Mission

The United Methodist Church still affirms that itineracy was

> from beginning to end, a *missional strategy.* . . . It was Methodism's mission to take the Gospel to those too poor to pay for it, too ignorant to appreciate its value, and not desiring it. And the itinerant system was the method by which to do it.[7]

In contrast are the frank comments of a prominent district superintendent in one of the larger Annual Conferences of the church: "The appointment system as it operates among us falls far short of the missional ideal. Very little time and energy are spent in the appointment process along the lines of deployment for mission, namely, local church missional needs and a pastor's missional gifts and skills." Another superintendent notes: "The lack of a clear articulated missional basis for itineracy is eroding it from within as nothing else! Too often pastors are given no clear missional reason for the appointments they receive. Pastors usually have to push for an answer to the question 'why?' " And an experienced Midwestern pastor observes that "most of us itinerant clergy don't have a sense of excitement about the church's mission being carried out through the appointment system."

In talking with seminarians and younger clergy I find a new spirit of inquiry into appointment making. For this group, appeals to service are empty without reference to specific place, context, needs, and goals. These newcomers respond to clergy and congregational profiles and the meshing of the two. Growing up in a time of church decline may have prompted their probing questions. One thing is certain: if we cannot tell them "why," we fail them and the church. Their inquiry points to the mission of the church.

It is obvious that if appointments are not made for clearly articulated missional reasons (replete with needs and goals), other factors will dominate the itinerant system. If missional appointments are not made in the normal course of appointment making but instead are seen as "exceptional," then the historic rationale for the itinerant system is denied, and the system becomes the servant of other forces.

At a recent national roundtable on the itineracy there was consensus that itineracy functions continually on four levels: (a) *a theological level* where there is concern and discussion about the missional needs of the church and how specific appointments can best respond to those needs; (b) *an administrative level* where statistics and problems are the focus of the process so that everyone can be fitted in; (c) *a value level* where salaries and benefits are the driving force behind appointments; (d) *a cultural level* that assumes that contemporary life-styles and career expectations simply are not open to appeals for sacrifice and self-denial, however demanding missional needs may be in specific appointment situations.

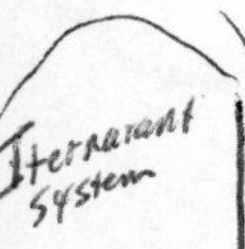

After moving through the Annual Conferences of the denomination for more than a decade, one is struck by the wide diversity in how the itinerant system functions. The painful conclusion is that the four levels cited above need to be listed in different sequences to get a realistic view of how itineracy functions in seventy-two conferences. Ideally, the theological and missional levels should claim primacy. However, in reality, the itineracy is most often understood as an administrative system driven primarily by salary scales and based on the assumption that the cultural norms of success and self-worth determine what is possible within the system. It is not too extreme to say that in the connection, the itinerant system is operating without a theology to sustain it, without a clear sense of mission to inspire it, and without a foundation of basic commitment to make it as effective as it was, and as it should be going into the twenty-first century.

The wonderful days of yesteryear in the itinerant system are easily romanticized, while senior bishops attest to great problems that have arisen in recent years due to the weakening of missional concerns. One retired bishop observes: "Twenty years ago retired bishops saw much of their fulfillment in having had the opportunity to fix appointments. Today they attest to being relieved in not having to do it any more." Itineracy, once an opportunity, has become a burden.

A prominent African-American pastor sincerely laments the current lack of excitement and enthusiasm that once characterized itineracy in the former Central Jurisdiction. Appointments were made and accepted with a missional sense that highlighted the original call to preach and to engage the world in the name of Jesus Christ, a hunger to serve undiminished by dozens of reservations and qualifications.

In the past decade no word in United Methodism has been more widely used and abused than "mission." If everything that is attempted is called missional; if the key to getting program after program adopted is to label it "missional"; if "mission" becomes trivialized into everyday jargon to justify and accommodate almost any program, it is small wonder that the mission of the church has lost much of its power and vitality. A magnet once able to draw laity and clergy to clearly articulated goals and objectives has become so diluted that it no longer carries the challenge and conviction that once elicited commitment.

Is there one mission of The United Methodist Church? Or are there 72 concepts of mission for 72 Annual Conferences; or 37,514 views of mission, one for each local church? Or is there room for 37,587 concepts of mission as long as they are rooted in the scriptural foundations of our Wesleyan heritage?

The 1984 General Conference sought to address this question with a Study Commission on the Mission of the Church, whose report was adopted at the 1988 General Conference. Similarly in 1984 and 1988 a Study Commission on the Ministry of the Church was appointed and continued at least through 1992. Because mission precedes ministry, the interest of the denomination in the two commissions and their reports is in sharp contrast. We began a study of the ministry, including itineracy, before we had determined the mission for which that ministry exists and is ordered and deployed. We continue to focus on a study of ministry with the expectation that it will be the focal point of the 1992 General Conference. How many bishops, district superintendents, local church pastors, lay leaders, and congregations have engaged in a study of the Mission Statement adopted in 1988? As of this writing, almost three years after its adoption, barely 2,000 copies are in circulation.

If it is to be more than just another management system, itineracy must indeed be "redeemed and renewed." Part of that redemption and renewal must be well-defined, clearly stated, and continuously focused missional goals and strategies. Some may say it is adequate to speak of "God's mission" or the Great Commission of Matthew 28:19-20. If this is true, we should need no exposition of the scriptures in preaching and teaching to make the gospel relevant and responsive to specific issues and concerns at every level of the church.

District superintendents have been charged in recent years to work with ministers and charge conferences "in formulating statements of purpose for congregations in fulfilling their mission" that inform profiles "reflecting the needs, characteristics and opportunities for mission of each pastoral appointment in the connection, such profiles to be reviewed annually and updated."[8] Many Annual Conferences have developed missional statements which project specific current and future needs for that area. What actual use is made of these definitions and descriptions of mission in deployment practices across the connection? Are these understandings of mission continually in the forefront as appointments are made? Is each appointment explained and justified in terms of goals and objectives set by laity and clergy at the grassroots level? Do cabinets have mission statements of their own wherein they commit themselves to their tasks within these goals?

It is encouraging that discussion toward consensus on these questions has taken place in some jurisdictional colleges of bishops. The Council of Bishops needs to discuss fully a church-wide strategy on missional appointments. One bishop has expressed the conviction that the question of ministerial appointments has become so serious that it should be on the agenda of every council meeting. Perhaps the annual inquiry of bishops concerning implementation of the consultation process could be enlarged into ongoing consideration of redeeming and renewing the itineracy system.

In relating itineracy more closely to the missional needs of the church, more than lip service must be paid to the principle of connectionalism. The 1988 Episcopal Address affirmed the problem:

> We need to find ways to make connectionalism come alive in the minds and hearts of the large percentage of our members for whom it is only a word. They need to catch the vision of being a part of a great adventure on behalf of Christ and Christ's mission. We are going to be a more connectional church, and what is more, the average lay person in the pews is going to know that and be excited about it, and that can revolutionize our mission.[9]

It is unlikely this will occur unless something happens to improve the purpose of Annual Conference sessions. Historically the power and influence of the Annual Conference has been inestimable. It was for Wesley and his ministers a true "*confer*"-*ence* when issues were

Annual Conf. just business

debated and actions taken by members who were informed biblically and theologically. In the interest of efficiency and saving money, the sessions in recent years have been so curtailed and streamlined that apart from appropriate worship moments, they differ little from secular business meetings. It is instructive to compare the current conference journals with those of a generation ago. Today they are thicker in pages but thinner in depth and substance. Statistical reports abound; records of spirited, informed debate and inspired sermons and lectures do not.

In this arena, where laity and clergy could engage in real missional planning and dialogue, precious opportunities have been squandered in order to get in and out as fast as possible. Instead of imagination and inspiration, indifference is frequently the result. The symbol of too many Annual Conferences is not the historic *"confer"-ence* between laity and clergy but the consent calendar, upon which more than just history is sinking. The savings in dollars compared to our loss amounts to questionable stewardship.

If missional criteria for appointments are not clarified, articulated, and demonstrated, itineracy will increasingly be dominated by other factors, which we discuss in the next section.

Challenges and Opportunities

Salaries and seniority. With the erosion of a strong theological base (the covenant) and the absence of a missional outlook to direct it (connectionalism), the itinerant system is easy prey to forces that blunt its fulfilling power and creative strategy. In the national roundtable discussion on itineracy referred to earlier, in representative conversations especially held for writing this chapter, and in hundreds of personal conversations over the years, there is no question that salaries and *seniority* are the most widespread and persistent challenges to a missional itinerant system. I emphasize *seniority* to note that we are not necessarily equating seniority with the experience that deepens commitment and sharpens clergy skills. It is just as possible for a person to have the same singular experience for twenty years in itineracy as it is to have a variety of different experiences in far less time. The seniority that is an obstacle to missional itineracy is synonymous with favoritism or "the good ol' boy network," undergirded by the supervisory philosophy that says "Don't mess up and you'll move up," to which pastors expectantly respond: "I'll never take a cut but always move up in salary."

Where salaries and seniority dominate itineracy to the point of idolatry, missional appointments are nearly impossible. The salary rankings are the starting point; cabinets work above and below them. Clergy are easily hooked by this monetary interpretation of itineracy. Cabinet members usually expect this ranking to be followed upon their leaving the superintendency. Rigid materialistic values within the system tend to label a lateral move or one for less salary (as missional appointments may need to be) as punitive. After a series of appointments within such an environment, clergy begin to view their self-worth and evaluate their effectiveness in terms of income. When an appointment is proposed for missional reasons, such an exception to business as usual is greeted with skepticism instead of enthusiasm. This skepticism is heightened by the fact that an appointment based on pastoral skills and experience matched with well-defined goals in a specific location will usually lead to a longer pastorate than the average tenure for ordained elders across the connection.[10] Shorter pastorates in the first half of one's career are necessary when salary is the driving force of itineracy. Consequently, there is pressure to move for advantage, and for position on the ladder.

Pastors across the denomination admit confidentially that they are weary of the competition in this kind of distorted itineracy. They see self-giving pastors in missional situations as unappreciated and not empowered by a system that misled them. This warning of weariness should be seen as an opportunity to redeem and renew itineracy.

The laity are increasingly unwilling to do business as usual under the itineracy system. Through the consultation process they have an opportunity to contribute to making appointments for missional reasons. The consultation that involves the Pastor-Parish Relations Committee should take into serious account the specific missional needs of each appointment. Although advisory, their role is active, not passive as in the days of mere notification. If consultation is authentic and laity feel they have been appropriately heard, they are supportive of the itinerant system. If consultation is not a serious process, congregational "call" tendencies are aroused. This attitude is increasingly true in a culture where people sense that they are losing their voice in government, education, medical care, and so on. The church increasingly becomes the one place where they expect their voices to be heard and taken seriously.

Without an apologetic for a missional itineracy in place, clearly interpreted for laity and clergy, and demonstrated throughout the appointment process, the basic integrity of itineracy becomes a most urgent and complex question. It is complex because of the layers of self-interest, personal relationships, and quiet unwritten assumptions that obscure its heart and genius. When, like mission, itineracy is talked about in idealistic terms but implemented in less than ideal ways, the integrity issue is unavoidable.

Solutions? There are no quick fixes since the vested interest in the salary-and-seniority-driven system is overwhelming. (This system is also more easily managed.) Equalization of salaries has an honorable history in world Methodism and in early American Methodism. It continues to emerge as an illusive ideal supposedly unrealistic for the American scene (a subtle capitulation to cultural norms).

One major objection to equalization of salaries that I have heard for years is that it encourages and harbors mediocrity. (The current system is similarly criticized.) This is easily assumed in the absence of any real models to the contrary. Having studied itineracy in British Methodism I find no factual basis for such an assumption. The question is whether The United Methodist Church in the United States is more a victim of cultural captivity than our sisters and brothers in Britain. Also, the British limitation on the length of an appointment has much to commend it. Their system has an evaluation component to determine the extension of appointment from five to nine years, up to a maximum of fourteen years. This process would bring consistency to an itineracy where limits on tenure apply to denominational executives (bishops, district superintendents, general agency secretaries) but not to an elite group of pastors where salaries dominate the system.

In his 1988 Episcopal Address Bishop Jack M. Tuell cited the salary issue as a basic obstacle to renewing the itineracy. Like others who find a need for change, he referred to the basic salary plan that was once open to Annual Conferences. Rarely used, the 1976 General Conference removed it as an option. In private conversations on itineracy this rejected option or some variation of it is often mentioned as worthy of consideration. Has itineracy become so inhibited by salary scales over these fifteen years that the option should be restored? Obviously, this option treads in sacrosanct precincts. Therefore, the easiest way to deal with it is to deny Annual Conferences the opportunity to consider it in any form. Bishop Tuell offered a creative suggestion worthy of far more attention than it has received:

> We face a situation in some annual conferences where the setting of pastoral salaries is being used as a way to step out of the appointive system. Although the authority to set salary rests with the charge conference, the danger of a rampant congregationalism here must be recognized. One legislative approach which might at least ameliorate the situation could be a disciplinary provision requiring a local congregation which wanted to raise its pastor's salary beyond a certain level to do so only if it committed an equal amount (over and above its apportionments) to the Equitable Salary Fund.[11]

An Equitable Salary Fund enlarged in this way is pure connectionalism. "The essence of a connectional system is that every church is part of every other church, and that no one church can live to itself alone."[12] This proposal would lessen the disparities and inequities where salary-driven itineracy prevails; would provide supplemental funds beyond minimum salary for appointments more missional than ordinary, and would foster a climate where further creative attention could be given to this urgent and complex issue.

Dual careers. Itineracy has always created stress in marriage and family life since it required mobility not inherent in most professions. Enforced mobility along with the need to accept an appointment determined by others meant genuine strains within parsonage life. Although increasingly adaptable to the requirements of semi-settled family life by the mid-nineteenth century, itineracy has continued to be marked by what one observer in a *Quarterly Review* of 1866 called "constant changes and restless energy."[13]

The changes and restlessness of a century ago have been quickened by the phenomenon of the working spouse in recent times. Some estimates place the percentage of spouses employed in the general population to be over 70 percent. Estimates of clergy spouses employed outside the home are not systematically calculated, but this group represents the majority of partners. When the prevailing model of itineracy operative in an Annual Conference is that of the spouse not working outside the home or not committed to that work as a vocational call, further conflict is added to the "constant changes and restless energy." It is especially acute when the spouse claims his or her vocational call to be as significant, meaningful, and divinely based as the spouse's call to ordained ministry, which in United Methodism in the United States has also meant the call to travel.

There is much cabinet frustration over clergy/spouse expectations in the resolving of the tensions of dual careers and calling.

Historically, bishops and cabinets have been sensitive to circumstances of family health and education. The new phenomenon of dual careers is hard to appreciate unless one is part of it, a classic example of a generational gap in expectations. Many congregations do not handle the situation well, since it is not part of their expectations of a parsonage family. If the response to this new and growing situation is confrontational, with pressures exerted and ultimatums presented, points may be scored on behalf of itineracy but no one wins, least of all the effective ministry of the church. If itineracy is to be redeemed and renewed, confrontation and conflict must give way to prevention and informed pragmatism, virtues not unknown to historic itineracy.

We have already alluded to the great need for better understanding of the expectations and obligations of the itinerant system. It is an understanding that should occur in the earlier stages of candidacy as provided in *The Book of Discipline* (Par. 404.1[4]). To counsel candidates about their call to ministry in The United Methodist Church without exploring with them the nature of the itinerant system, the ministerial covenant and the connectional principle, and the expectations and obligations of both the church and the pastors is one of the worst forms of ecclesiastical neglect and malpractice. To explore the issue at this early stage, even to press it with intensity, is a fair and just part of church authentication of an individual's sense of call, as well as an intrinsic factor in the qualifying process. To delay this important discussion until a later stage, such as the first full-time appointment or the first change in appointment, is unfair and weakening to the itineracy system at its foundations.

Local church pastors, pastor-parish relations committees, district committees, and Annual Conference Boards of Ordained Ministry and cabinets are required to take the initiative in this area. Through the counseling and supervisory activities of these bodies adequate understanding of itineracy will provide the basis for important decisions to be made by a dual-career couple.

However the system seeks to accommodate the vocational situations of dual-career couples, ultimately it is a personal family matter to come to terms with the expectations and obligations of itineracy. It should be clear that it is beyond the scope of any deployment system to resolve vocational situations and make vocational decisions for mature adult couples. Itineracy cannot resolve all the demands and expectations placed upon it from any quarter and remain itineracy—"disciplined and directed mobility"—a kind of team ministry created by and for the ministry as a whole.[14] When couples have negotiated and arrived at personal career decisions, they can inform the bishop and cabinet, who can seek to accommodate that decision as far as reasonable itineracy allows. This process is far more responsible than expecting the cabinet to resolve the career conflicts and then complaining, "They made us do it."

The couple must commit themselves to living out the consequences of their career decision, which may mean that for the clergy member not all the opportunities that would be available for him or her under full mobility will be possible. In fairness to the connection and other pastors in the covenant, the couple should not expect to stay unduly long in one appointment, even under limited mobility, since a system that serves personal convenience above all else is not United Methodist itineracy.

Ineffective pastors. A generation ago Horace Greeley Smith, writing on the itinerant ministry in the famous volume *Methodism,* edited by William K. Anderson, observed: "A point at which our itinerant system seems almost completely stymied is in dealing with the case of the [person] who is ineffective."[15] In that era the usual method of dealing with ineffectiveness in itineracy was to move the pastor frequently, often at a distance from the previous appointment, and to hope for the best. Rarely was the best realized, and the pastoral record of ineffective pastors became extended.

Using itineracy for therapeutic purposes is doomed to failure, for rarely does a change in geography change reality or call forth hidden clergy gifts and skills. The price for this misuse of itineracy is incredible. This practice is unfair to effective clergy who are inhibited by problems created by others. The ineffective pastors receive cruel punishment instead of covenantal care, as their self-worth and the happiness of their families diminishes from one impossible appointment to another. Itineracy is discredited at every level.

Predicting effectiveness is very difficult. Persons may meet the qualifications, but when appointed to full-time ministry may prove not to have the "gifts and graces" of which they and their counselors were convinced. The candidacy process of The United Methodist Church is the most thorough among mainline denominations, but it is no better than those persons charged with administering it. Increased commitment to the time, energy, and skill that candidacy supervision requires is incumbent upon laity in the local churches, the pastors of candidates, pastors and lay observers on district committees and boards of ordained ministry, supervising pastors who are the personal mentors of candidates, and upon the district superintendents who supervise the parish work prior to full connection. Bishops, district superintendents, and others charged with nominating persons to these key roles need to be sensitive to the duties and responsibilities of these positions, including the mandate to say no when they are convinced that a candidate will not perform effective ministry.

The initial full-time appointment is crucial for future effective ministry, a fact that cannot be emphasized too strongly. First appointments should be in places where colleagueship is readily available. Experience reveals that the ineffective pastor is often a loner who has been working (struggling) outside the covenant from the time of the initial appointment. Many who leave itineracy do so in the first five years. British Methodists have long recognized the strategic importance of this first pastoral appointment. As long as the tradition of isolating pastors in their first appointment prevails, the more difficult it becomes to offer the "ineffective pastor in the making" the supervisory and collegial support he or she must have.

Some conferences are intentional about clergy support groups, a development we would do well to encourage more evenly across the church. Such colleague groups cannot be programmed, or they will lose their open and voluntary nature and be viewed more as a requirement than as an opportunity. But they can be encouraged by boards of ordained ministry and district superintendents and modeled by these official groups which take the initiative to embody the covenant spirit.

No denomination has placed a higher value on constructive supervision, evaluation, and continuing education than United Methodism. For more than a decade, a primary basis of continuing appointment has been "annual participation in evaluation with Committees on Pastor-Parish Relations for use in ongoing effective ministry," as well as "growth in competence and effectiveness through continuing education."[16] When boards of ordained ministry and cabinets understand the relationship between evaluation and continuing education, and provide criteria, procedures, and training that are neither threatening nor impracticable, and make funds available for continuing education, the enhancement of skills for effective ministry is probable for a number of pastors in every Annual Conference. Left without these support services, these pastors might spend their unexamined careers itinerating in circles of personal disappointment and dissatisfied congregations.

For many years bishops, cabinets, and boards of ordained ministry shared the frustration of being almost completely stymied in dealing with ineffective pastors. In direct response to their frustration, the procedure for administrative location was introduced into the itinerant system in 1980 and has been revised in the interest of relevance, feasibility, and fairness to pastors.[17] A special General Conference Committee will offer further strengthening of this option to the 1992 General Conference. This procedure requires cooperation between boards and cabinets. It requires making the judgment that a minister has demonstrated an inability to perform effective ministry. It requires the ministerial covenant to function compassionately, and even to consider financial assistance during the transition from itineracy. But it does require *initiative* to be taken when supportive efforts have failed. To date, this option in dealing with ineffective pastors has been surprisingly under-used in the light of the church-wide request for just such a procedure. The opportunity is in place, but without initiative, congregations, pastors, and the itinerant system will not be served.

This chapter has sought to address some of the complex questions urgently facing itineracy. It has done so in the firm conviction that historic, pragmatic itineracy can carefully and creatively resolve these issues. "Fully recognizing the stresses being placed upon the itineracy today and acknowledging there is much reforming work to be done, we nevertheless, in the name and for the sake of our common mission, commit ourselves to a renewed itineracy."[18]

The church waits.

PART II: SOCIAL AND MISSIONAL CHALLENGES

CHAPTER 6

Who Is the Client? The Clergy or the Congregation?

Lyle E. Schaller

In recent years the public schools in the United States have been subjected to careful and repeated scrutiny. One approach evaluates the system from the perspective of the teachers and raises questions about morale, pensions, training, salaries, tenure, and similar issues. Others have focused on what happens to the children who are enrolled in the public schools. This second group asks questions about dropout rates, scores on standardized tests, moral and ethical behavior, academic skills, pregnancy rates, drug use, preparation for entry into the labor force, and similar concerns.

One of the differences between these two approaches is in the identification of the client. The first begins with the teachers as the principal client, the second assumes that the students represent the primary client.

A dialogue on the United Methodist system of ministerial placement begins with a parallel question. Who is the primary client? The Annual Conference? The theological seminaries that produce the graduates for the system? The denomination as a whole? The cabinet? The pastors? The churches?

Is Itinerancy the Issue?

Occasionally someone identifies short pastorates as the distinctive characteristic of American Methodism. This was a valid observation many years ago. Of the graduates of Yale College between 1702 and 1775 who entered the congregational ministry, 79 percent spent their entire pastoral career in one congregation while another 14 percent served only two congregations.[1] A great many Lutheran and Reformed pastors in the eighteenth and nineteenth centuries devoted their entire adult lives to serving only one parish. By contrast, the itinerant United Methodist preacher moved frequently. For many, six months in one place was the maximum.

Today nearly all Protestant pastors itinerate. Most denominations report somewhere between 10 percent and 35 percent of all pastor-parish relationships are terminated during the average year. Most United Methodist conferences report that figure is between 15 percent and 25 percent. Perhaps as many as one-third of all first pastorates and of all circuit arrangements are terminated every year, but United Methodism now varies only slightly from other Protestant traditions in the average length of pastorates.

The main difference between the United Methodist ministerial placement system and other Protestant traditions is that this denomination has retained the Roman Catholic system whereby ministers are sent by a bishop rather than called by a congregation as they are in nearly all other Protestant bodies.

The Clergy as Clients

If one views the clergy as the primary client of this system of ministerial placement, much can be said in its favor. Ministers from other denominations frequently express considerable envy about six facets of our system.

Bishops and denominational executives in other Protestant traditions often wish they had similar authority when the situation demands a particular pastor be moved as soon as possible. In many traditions that requires months or years. In this denomination it can be and has been accomplished within forty-eight hours, often with no career damage to that pastor.

Clergy couples from other traditions also express envy for this system which often offers "the trailing spouse" an acceptable appointment without months of frustrating delay. In some conferences the placement of clergy couples has become a high priority in the annual appointment process.

Perhaps the greatest amount of envy is expressed by pastors in other Protestant traditions who have been dismissed by their congregations over issues such as incompetence, immorality, substance abuse, divorce, social action, poor preaching, personality clashes, laziness, or doctrinal stance. Sometimes the dismissal is effective immediately, and only one or two months of terminal leave compensation accompany that dismissal. These pastors, many of whom are never able to re-enter the parish ministry, envy the job security of United Methodist pastors.

Ordained women in other Protestant traditions also look with envy at how easily their United Methodist sisters are able to move to their second pastorate. That first call is becoming easier to find, but that second or third call often requires many years of patient waiting in the other denominations that ordain women.

A fifth source of envy by some pastors is the relatively generous pension program of United Methodists. While the benefit-based system is now being phased out, the United Methodist pastor who retires in 1992 after forty years of service can expect an annual pension of $8,000 to $12,000 in most Annual Conferences, thanks to the increases in that rate to offset the impact of inflation. In most traditions, both Protestant and Roman Catholic, forty years of pastoral service yields a far smaller annual pension.

Finally, thousands of bivocational pastors in other traditions who continue in a full-time secular job to enable them to serve a congregation averaging 35 to 85 at Sunday morning worship envy their United Methodist colleagues who are guaranteed a minimum (or equitable) salary by their Annual Conference while serving a small church.

In addition, the United Methodist system is also a comfortable security blanket for (a) the pastor who wears out his or her welcome after a year or two and is forced to move; (b) the pastor who feels a deep sense of God's call to the pastoral ministry, but whose competence does not match that commitment; (c) the weary or lazy or "burned out" fifty-seven-year-old pastor who is "playing out the string until retirement"; (d) the district superintendent or conference staff member who is now due to re-enter the pastorate, but does not have to search for a call; and (e) ministers who have been on a leave of absence for several years and want to return to the pastoral ministry.

A Distinctive Downside

While it is seldom seen by the participants as other than a rare incident, the United Methodist system of ministerial placement has made scores of senior ministers into victims.

The typical scenario begins when an associate minister is appointed to a large congregation by the cabinet, rather than selected by the senior pastor. As the weeks and months roll by, it becomes apparent that this is an incompatible match. As the tensions become more apparent, the Staff-Parish Committee intervenes. Rather than risk being accused of playing favorites, this committee often recommends to the cabinet that both ministers be replaced.

While this scenario is also played out in other traditions, it is very unusual. One reason, of course, is that the senior pastor either chooses every program staff member or has a highly influential voice in making that decision. A second reason is that the simple alternative of replacing both pastors is not that tempting in other traditions. A third reason is that the office of senior pastor is usually held in higher esteem in other Protestant traditions.

From a larger perspective this scenario illustrates what many observers contend is the unique flaw in our system. Instead of facing up to the need to resolve conflict in a healthy manner, this system tempts leaders to avoid it by changing appointments. This is an especially serious issue in the circulation of "problem pastors" or incompetent ministers from one congregation to another, often accompanied by a conference financial subsidy. This is *not* a feature of our system that is widely envied by leaders from other denominations! They believe it is wiser to face the issue than to avoid it.

What Is the Reward System?

While it is far from universal, the heart of the reward system for pastors in other traditions is usually based on a combination of faithfulness, competence, experience, personality, and productivity. These are the characteristics high on the list of nearly every pulpit nominating committee as they seek a new pastor.

Denominational executives from other traditions repeatedly express amazement at the degree to which our system is driven by salary. To be more precise, the system is designed to reward the pastor who is effective in persuading the congregation to raise the salary.

On rare occasions the pastor who wants to move may also improve that statistical record by reporting exaggerated numbers to the conference journal. This discrepancy will be discovered by the successor eventually, but the predecessor has already been "promoted."

From a congregational perspective, the most distinctive characteristic of the reward system has expanded tremendously during the past quarter century. This takes the form of a variety of financial subsidies to smaller congregations. In the eyes of leaders in large congregations, this reward system has two facets: (1) large congregations with a high level of member giving are asked to divert the funds that could be used to employ one or two additional program staff members to pay the apportionments, and (2) these funds are redirected as subsidies to enable small churches to have a full-time resident pastor. This Robin Hood role for the Annual Conference (a) rewards the underemployed pastor, (b) punishes the highly productive program staff in the larger churches by increasing their workload, (c) rewards the churches with a low level of stewardship, (d) taxes the churches with a high level of stewardship, (e) rewards a numerical shrinkage in size, (f) taxes numerical growth, (g) redirects funds from congregations with the potential for numerical growth to congregations with limited potential for growth, (h) helps to explain the rapid increase in the number of small and numerically shrinking congregations (numerical growth and long-term financial subsidies are mutually incompatible), (i) helps to explain the net decrease of over two million in membership since 1965, (j) helps to explain the decrease in the number of larger congregations, and (k) helps to explain the recent increase in the number of pastoral charges from 24,268 in 1973 to 25,840 in 1989—despite a net decrease of 1,500 in the number of congregations and a net loss of 1.4 million members during those sixteen years. (Economists agree that whatever is taxed will decrease in numbers while whatever is subsidized will increase.) This redistribution of income from understaffed large churches to underemployed pastors may be the most distinctive feature of the United Methodist system of ministerial placement!

Does the System Serve the Churches?

The past quarter century has seen at least a tripling in the number of Protestant congregations averaging more than five hundred at Sunday morning worship. This is the era of the large "seven-day-a-week" church. These congregations are especially attractive to the generations born after 1945. Between 1965 and 1988 the number of United Methodist congregations averaging over five hundred at worship has dropped by one-third from 757 to 516. Have our large churches been well served by this system of ministerial placement?

In 1980 this denomination reported 21,725 United Methodist congregations that included 200 or fewer members. Eight years later, 69 percent of these congregations had shrunk in size, and only 31 percent reported an increase of at least 1 percent in membership. A total of 1,928 reported that their membership had declined by 50 percent or more, while only 600 reported a net growth of at least 50 percent.[2] Have these shrinking small churches been well served by this system?

The merger of 1968 was followed by the closing or merging of more than 3,000 congregations. By 1974, however, most of these "adjustments" had been completed. Between 1974 and 1988 the number of United Methodist congregations averaging fewer than 35 at worship increased by more than 1,000 while those averaging 35 to 149 at worship decreased from 21,097 to 19,782. The number averaging 150 to 349 decreased from 5,595 to 4,884. Have these churches been well served by this system? (It also should be asked whether this decrease in the number of larger congregations has been beneficial to those pastors who want to move from a smaller congregation to a larger one.)

The viability of circuits has come under widespread review in recent years. The basic generalization is that being part of a circuit increases the probability a small church will either be closed or merged. Have these churches been well served by a system that creates circuits to "make a salary"?

For a denomination to remain on a plateau in size, the number of newly organized churches each year should be at least equal to 1 percent of all congregations in that denomination. The fast-growing denominations have set and implemented goals of 2 or 3 percent as part of a denomination-wide church growth strategy.

The number of new congregations organized each decade by The United Methodist Church and its six predecessor denominations has dropped from over 7,400 (1.5 percent per year) during the 1880s to 2,000 (0.5 percent per year) during the 1950s to 800 (0.2 percent per year) during the 1980s. At least eight times as much money is spent each year subsidizing appointments for pastors in long established congregations as is spent on new church development. Has the denominational new church development program been well served by this system of ministerial placement?

One of the biblical imperatives for the churches is to "make disciples." The number of new members received by confession of faith has dropped from 385,000 as recently as 1960 to 186,000 in 1988.

Thus back in 1960 the average congregation in the two predecessor denominations received nine new members by confession of faith. That figure had dropped to five in 1988. The total number of baptisms dropped from 440,000 for the two predecessor denominations in 1956 to 338,000 in 1964 to 200,000 in 1980 to 170,000 in 1988. Has that evangelistic imperative been well served by this system of ministerial placement?

From an institutional survival rate, the most ominous pair of statistics is found in death rates. In 1952 the former Methodist Church reported the annual death rate of members was 8.8 per 1,000 members. That was far below the death rate of 11.4 per 1,000 United States citizens, age 14 and over, in 1952. By 1988 the death rate for this denomination had climbed to 13.9 per 1,000 members while the death rate in the United States, age 14 and over, had dropped to 10.9. Is the future of this denomination being well served by this system of ministerial placement?

A key to reaching the generations born after 1945 is a strong teaching ministry. Nearly everyone who has studied that subject agrees that the pastor is the key person in building an attractive teaching ministry. The average attendance in our Sunday schools has plunged from 4.1 million in 1962 for the two predecessor denominations to under 2 million in 1988. Sunday school attendance in the average church in 1962 was 98, but had dropped to 52 in 1988. Have our Sunday schools been well served by the present system of ministerial placement?

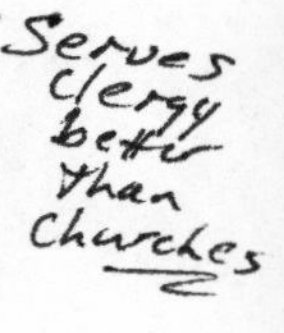

This is not intended to be an exhaustive appraisal, but it demonstrates that the present system serves the clergy better than it serves the churches. If that is the primary goal, nothing more needs to be said. But a growing number of people, both lay and clergy, contend the system isn't working.

Where to Begin?

In several Annual Conferences the beginning point reflects the conclusion that no one is in charge here. The organizational structure is dysfunctional. It has become impossible to build a consensus in support of a strategic plan or a narrowly focused set of priorities in the allocation of resources.

One possibility currently being discussed would be to create an executive committee chaired by a lay volunteer. This committee would be the final source of all recommendations to come before that

Annual Conference on the allocation of scarce resources. This committee would be responsible for assuring that all recommendations on the allocation of resources were consistent with the long-term strategic plan and priorities of that conference. This would require (a) creating and adopting a conference strategy and set of priorities,[3] (b) funneling all recommendations from conference committees that involve the allocation of scarce resources (money, staff time, assignment of pastors, building space, camps, etc.) through this committee, (c) transforming the reward system described earlier so it would be compatible with the conference strategy and priorities, and (d) approving a radical change in the redistribution of power.

Conversations with leaders, both lay and clergy, from large congregations indicate that they believe this scenario could not be adopted by any Annual Conference. As a result, these leaders are concentrating their time, energy, creativity, and other resources on strengthening the ministry and outreach of their congregation. This is most readily visible in the efforts of those churches that are effectively implementing a vision to grow younger and larger.

A few of these leaders have concluded that remedial action will initially require changing the system of representation in decision-making circles. Currently Annual Conferences are designed to provide voting rights to (a) the clergy and (b) representatives of congregations. That system probably makes it impossible for conferences to adopt an action plan that will either (a) threaten the security and benefits of the clergy or (b) threaten the direct and indirect financial subsidies now enjoyed by many of the congregations.

One proposal, for example, would be to change to a system that represents people. Every one thousand members would be entitled to one ministerial and one lay delegate to Annual Conference. Congregations with a combined membership of one thousand would choose one ministerial and one lay delegate. The three-thousand member church would be entitled to three lay and three ministerial delegates.

What chance do you believe that design has for adoption in the typical Annual Conference?

The most common response has been to create a special committee that will tinker with the existing machinery in the hope of greater economy and efficiency. If the issue is systemic reform, these committees are certain both to arouse and to encounter high levels of frustration and opposition.

Four Other Scenarios

After more than three decades of working with more than fifty denominations, I offer four other scenarios. The first is based on a comparison of the United Methodist appointment system, which is modeled after the Roman Catholic system of ministerial placement, and the Methodist Church in Korea.

In preparation for the centennial celebration of Korean Methodism, the Koreans in the mid-1970s set a goal of doubling in a decade. They surpassed that goal, growing from approximately 400,000 to over one million members. To achieve it, they implemented a three-part strategy: (1) they organized hundreds of new missions; (2) they abolished the appointment process, thus enabling their bishops to serve as parish pastors with limited part-time episcopal responsibilities; and (3) they encouraged the emergence and growth of many very large congregations.

Implementation of this scenario in the United States would enable three dozen bishops to return to the pastorate; it would mean many ministers now being subsidized by the conference could become bivocational pastors; it would free up large sums of money for new church development; it would reduce the apportionment load on larger churches, thus enabling them to expand their program and outreach; and it would sharply reduce the number of committees required to staff the administrative structure of the Annual Conference.

Can The United Methodist Church switch from a Roman Catholic system of ministerial placement to an evangelical Protestant system?

If, instead of scrapping this inherited system of ministerial placement, a more modest goal is adopted to renew it and revitalize it, another scenario appears to be the most promising. This requires reversing the twenty-five years of growing older and smaller and seeking to reach and serve the generations born after 1955.

The pragmatic reason for this is simple. Numerically growing institutions display many advantages over numerically shrinking institutions. These include the capability to attract, promote, and keep highly qualified people, an acceptance of people who color outside the lines, the capability to focus on the needs of people rather than on institutional survival, an enthusiasm for creating a new tomorrow rather than seeking to recreate yesterday, a greater openness to creativity and innovation, and placing the top priority in the allocation of scarce resources on servicing the clientele rather than on taking care of the employees.

Unfortunately, this scenario may be impossible to implement without major systemic changes. One is a basic law of economics referred to earlier: whatever is subsidized increases while whatever is taxed decreases. The decision by most Annual Conferences to increase the apportionments for large congregations in order to subsidize smaller churches is a politically popular policy. Both the United States Congress and United Methodist conferences find it politically difficult to reduce financial subsidies once they are granted.

A second barrier for this scenario is that The United Methodist Church has drifted to the left of center of the theological spectrum, becoming a low-commitment religious body while the churchgoers born after 1955 clearly prefer high-commitment congregations, which are usually evangelical churches as well. That shift may be difficult to reverse in a denomination controlled by people born before 1955.

A third scenario is essentially political. This calls for candidates for the episcopacy to campaign on a platform promising elimination of the present ministerial placement system. Could they be elected? Have so many people become so dependent on the security guaranteed by the present system that these candidates could not be elected?

A fourth scenario, and one that might win substantial support, requires two changes. Both would be difficult to adopt. The first would be elimination of the guaranteed appointment. The cabinet would be authorized to give six months' notice to any pastor that an appointment will not be available to that minister at the next session of the Annual Conference. The delivery of such a notice to some pastors could cause such severe disruption that a back-up system would be required. This could be appointment of a pastor to a six-month transitional sabbatical which would include full compensation, counseling, retraining, and assistance in a job search. This could be financed out of funds now used to subsidize ministerial appointments.

If an average attendance at worship of 125 or more is required for a congregation to be (a) an economically viable appointment for a full-time conference member to provide a full work load, and (b) to constitute a challenging assignment, this would require 9,000 full conference members for the entire denomination, including conference staff, associate ministers, district superintendents, and bishops. That would require phasing out appointments for approximately 17,000 ministers and a huge reduction in subsidies.

Congregations averaging fewer than 125 at worship could be served by bivocational pastors, retirees, and ministers who want less than full-time compensation and other arrangements. (In 1965 the average church had an attendance of 100 at worship. In 1988 that average had dropped to 91.)

The second change required for this scenario grows out of the fact that in many Annual Conferences the pool of qualified candidates for a particular assignment is often limited to two to seven ministers. A radically different set of competencies is required of the person who is to be appointed to be the senior pastor of a megachurch than is required for a program director in a large church, or to be founding pastor of a new Korean mission, or to serve as the pastor of a stable congregation averaging 145 at worship in a small county seat, or to reverse the numerical decline of a suburban church founded in 1957. The old slogan that "any conference member can serve any appointment" is clearly obsolete. To be more precise, in an increasingly complicated and specialized society, the present system is producing far too many mismatches in which the newly appointed minister does not bring the gifts, skills, experience, personality, work habits, and training required for that particular assignment. These mismatches probably rank at the top of that list of reasons for the decrease in the number of large churches, for the aging and shrinkage of the total membership, and for that startling increase in the number of small congregations.

Thus the second change that this scenario calls for is shifting from that numerically limited conference pool of candidates for any one particular appointment to a national market. That shift should create a much larger pool of potential candidates, produce fewer mismatches, facilitate church growth strategies, reduce the number of ministers who move only because of the need to make the present system work, lengthen the tenure of the average pastorate, improve the possibilities for adequately staffing large congregations, create a broader range of choices for clergy couples, and raise morale.

It would cost money. Both the bishops and the superintendents would have to improve their level of competence as personnel officers. This would require a tremendous improvement in the quality of the data base available to the cabinet on both congregations and pastors. This change in the role of the superintendents should also be accompanied by removing the six-year limit in office on superintendents. The learning curve is real! This would mean professionalizing the placement process.

An alternative would be to adopt the current practices used by the Presbyterians, the United Church of Christ, Lutherans, and others, and move to a congregational call system for ministerial placement. This would enable at least four or five hundred of our most gifted and skilled clergy, who are now serving as superintendents and bishops, to move back into the parish ministry. That one change alone in the allocation of ministerial leadership might help to reverse the numerical decline of the past quarter century.

The major disadvantage of the congregational call system is that sometimes a good match between pastor and people in one congregation is disrupted when that contented pastor receives a challenging invitation to move. That also happens, however, in The United Methodist Church when a pastor who does not want to move and a congregation that does not want a change is faced with the demand for a new appointment in order to make the system work.

The Price of Reform Is High

This fourth scenario represents the most radical changes of any of the four. The first radical change would be a reversal of the past quarter century of encouraging an increase in the number of smaller congregations and a reduction in the number of larger churches by nurturing an increase in the number of congregations averaging more than 125 at worship. A second radical change would be to focus on supporting that one-fourth of all churches that includes two-thirds of the members. The current system is designed to support the three-quarters of churches that includes one-third of all members. Instead of sending resources where few people are present, this scenario places first priority on allocating resources where most of the people are located.

A third radical change would be to replace the present top priority of providing support to the clergy with a new priority of allocating support where numerical growth in membership is most likely to occur.

A fourth radical change would be the assumption that the Annual Conference exists for the benefit of the churches rather than the churches exist to support the Annual Conference.

From a ministerial perspective, the most radical facet of this scenario would be the sharp reduction in jobs for full-time conference members. Given the present system for voting delegates at Annual Conference, that threat could turn out to be the rallying point for defeat of this scenario.

This threat could be reduced by offering all congregations averaging under 125 at worship a range of alternatives. They would be free to choose from a long list of alternatives in securing ministerial leadership. Each congregation could be a part of a circuit if it could find partner churches for that arrangement, or seek a part-time or full-time resident pastor, or choose to be served by a non-resident part-time minister.

While the results cannot be guaranteed, this option of increasing local control might be a means of slowing the rate of numerical decline of these smaller churches, and of reducing the number of congregations that are closed every year. If only a few leaders are convinced that a crisis does exist, the attractive scenario for most will be to postpone all proposals for change until after "my term in office is over."

CHAPTER 7
A Generic Lay Perspective

Sally B. Geis

The Generic United Methodist

My role as this volume's only lay author, except for clergy spouses, is analogous to the role persons of color play in white society. People on the "inside," in this case the clergy, try to be considerate of those on the "outside," meaning the laity. Since outsiders are affected by decisions that insiders make, considerate insiders sometimes ask, "What do you people think?"

Friends who are not Euro-American have told me how frustrating this position can be. No one Native American, no one Jew, no one black South African can represent the diversity that exists within her or his group. Yet individual "outsiders" accept spokesperson roles when they believe that one voice is better than none, even if a single voice can never adequately represent a group.

Believing that any consideration of the itineracy needs to include a lay voice, I accepted the assignment, knowing that my thinking does not represent the thinking of all nine million United Methodists in the United States. The only justification for generalizing from my statements is that I am, by statistical standards, a generic United Methodist. I am Anglo (96 percent of us are), female (61 percent), and a United States citizen (89 percent).[1] Born into the denomination, I attended church in a small city in rural America. (Most of our churches are rural.) The paid staff consisted of a full-time clergyman, a woman who served as Christian education director-secretary, and the custodian from a nearby office building who shoveled snow in the winter and mowed the grass in the summer. (Most clergy serve single-pastor charges.)

Now I am middle-aged (only 9.7 percent of us are under 35) and live in an urban metropolitan area, as do most Americans. My husband and I attend a church served by four ordained persons, two diaconal ministers, and five other staff persons. (Thirty-three percent of us attend high-steeple churches.)

Our two children are just as typical of their generation as I am of mine. One son, along with his wife and two young children, attends a Presbyterian church because the Presbyterians have the best church school program in their city, and they want the children to have the best. (Denominational loyalty is no longer the strong tie that it once was.)

Our other son does not attend church regularly because he does not find what goes on there particularly relevant. He is not interested in whether we call God mother or father, nor in how we organize the church. He has decided that for now he can be more effective in finding housing for the homeless or saving the environment by working in secular organizations that address those problems directly.

As Tex Sample says in his recent book, *U.S. Lifestyles and Mainline Churches,* "In spite of all the publicity given to conservative and fundamentalist churches in recent years, they are not drawing any greater proportion of the population and are not reversing the trends in the United States."[2] Popular wisdom notwithstanding, the largest group of persons lost to The United Methodist Church are "disproportionately young, male, white, well educated, non-southerners, and frequent movers. They are less conformist on social issues and cultural attitudes and far more tolerant and open to change."[3] They are persons in their twenties, thirties, and early forties. "College-educated, cosmopolitan, affluent, middle-class young people who prize individual expression, freedom, autonomy and relativism simply left the churches."[4]

We middle-class Anglo United Methodists are losing our own children, not somebody else's. Their world views, which are informed by the faith their parents taught them, must be considered when we worry about membership loss and the future of the church. We must pay attention to both the lost sheep and the new lambs whom we wish to bring into the fold.

Images of the Past Shape Expectations of the Future

If the church is to respond adequately to those we have lost and to those yet unaffected by the faith it must listen attentively to voices from outside the walls as well as to the voice of an aging white generic member like me. Otherwise our numbers will continue to dwindle.

While acknowledging that the church cannot allow its ministry to be shaped by worldly concerns, we must also acknowledge that the church exists to serve the world *as it is.* Jesus lived and taught among the common people of his time, and as his servants we are called to do the same.

A hard look at today's world suggests that it is drastically different from the world in which I, the generic church member, grew to adulthood. However, our *interpretations* of today's world are filtered through images from our past that are powerful elements in shaping our understanding of the present and the future. It is my conviction that our method of clergy appointment was more appropriate in the society I knew as a child than in the one to which I now belong.

To be clear, I am not suggesting a general church task force to study the itineracy. Nor am I suggesting that we initiate major revisions on the general church level. Our church is already suffering from too much preoccupation with its structure and its formal definitions. All I ask is that we add some flexibility and take some risks with the system we have.

A traditional perspective on the clergy role. In what kind of world did the itinerant system as we know it function well? In the world of my childhood it seemed adequate.

All the clergy I ever knew were Anglo males. The clergy wives (and the clergy all had wives) were required to keep very clean houses, cook lots of food for church suppers, attend all women's society meetings, and dress neatly but not too fashionably.

The preacher's children were models of proper behavior for the rest of us. We also learned, however, that we did not really need to be as "goody two shoes" as the preacher's kids. We had more license to express our individuality and to spend our money on movies and drug store sodas. I never once envied anyone who was a preacher's kid.

The clergyman himself was to be treated a little like the policeman. You were told by your parents that he was there to help you, but you hoped fervently that you would never need his help. Even as a child I knew intuitively that a position of institutional authority included the ability to control and punish others. I never wanted to be in a position to "have a little talk" with either the policeman or the preacher. Nevertheless it gave me a sense of security to know that one was on the street corner and the other was in the pulpit monitoring behavior and keeping things the way they were supposed to be.

I did not focus on the role of the district superintendent until I was much older, but I knew about bishops from a very early age. The bishop was more like God than even our preacher because he was the one who sent us our preacher. Sometimes my mother, who was shockingly forthright in the eyes of some, dared to talk back to the bishop about what we wanted or needed. But deep down we all knew that in the end the bishop could have his way. The only reason for speaking up was to try to influence his thinking, not to challenge his power.

I cannot remember knowing a divorced clergyman or a single one. It never occurred to me that a woman could be clergy or that a clergyman's wife could work for pay, except maybe as church secretary if we did not pay the preacher enough to live on.

As I write this description I can hardly believe that it describes a reality I knew and took for granted, but it does. Our whole community, not just the Methodist Church, functioned within a normative framework that was white, male, and Christian dominated. The Christmas pageant was as much a part of the public school program as of the church's. (Only as an adult did I wonder how the three Jewish families in town felt about that.) Except for Mary, the important people in the pageant were all Anglo males, as were the mayor and city council, the teachers, and the policemen.

We must be careful not to oversimplify what this description teaches us about the itineracy. It is not enough to recruit women and persons of color into the ministry or to increase the number of cross-cultural appointments.

If cultural diversity becomes the norm within our church, no homogeneous generic treatment of either laity or clergy will suffice. Our understanding of cultural differences must deepen until its effects permeate the ministry and structure of the church in more ways than we now understand.

People from different backgrounds raise their children differently, spend their leisure time differently, learn differently. Many of us are familiar with the struggles of the generic public school to adapt to different cultural learning styles. Churches are experiencing the same confusion about the development of adequate responses to a multicultural society.

What changes will be required if the church learns to understand a reality in which people from different cultures worship differently, theologize differently, practice ministry differently? Probably no one of us can imagine all that it means, but we are interested in discerning some part of its meaning for the clergy appointment system in The United Methodist Church. All we can do is make an educated guess based on what we know about social structure and culture.

As we diversify, it will become more difficult for the church to recruit, train, and appoint as if all local churches have similar needs. In other words, the cabinet of a single Annual Conference can no longer treat clergy as if they were a homogeneous group, any one of whom could be appointed to any charge. The generic vision of clergy appointable anywhere functioned more adequately in our monolithic cultural past than it will in a multivaried cultural future. This observation is in no sense an apology for perpetuating a system of racially or ethnically segregated church appointments. Objections to clergy appointments based on stereotypical assumptions about those characteristics is prejudice and has no place in the church.

Pluralism has a broad and complex meaning in today's world. It includes generational differences, class differences, and rural and urban differences that are frequently more important than race or ethnicity. An adequate understanding of diversity will prompt the church to analyze the cultural milieu of our communities and adapt its recruitment, mentoring, and placement of clergy.

Accommodation Has Already Begun

One significant adaptation has already taken place—namely, the addition of the consultative process as part of appointment making. A description of the major areas of cultural diffusion that brought about this adaptation are instructive to our analysis.

1. *Changes in family structure and life-style.* These hardly need to be enumerated, they are so familiar to clergy and laity alike. Divorce, blended families, working mothers, single parents are common patterns in today's church and world.

The clergypersons in my life today are as typical as the ones of my childhood, but they are also very different. Some of our bishops are divorced or remarried and members of blended families. District superintendents' life-styles vary. One may be a divorced or widowed woman who supports dependent children; another may be a partner in a clergy couple.

Local church clergy are equally diverse. Many have spouses who work in secular occupations; some came into the ministry as young persons directly out of college and seminary; others are second-career persons or women who went to seminary after raising their children.

2. *Greater racial and gender inclusiveness.* All clergy, from bishops to new deacons, now come from many ethnic origins. The gender balance is changing. The number of clergywomen in The United Methodist Church has increased 122 percent between 1981 and 1989.[5] They permeate the structure as bishops, district superintendents, and local church pastors, as well as holding special appointments.

3. *Changes in the mix brought changes in power distribution.* The good news is that the current appointment system has been flexible enough to nurture and place persons from a wide variety of backgrounds. The bad news is that without even greater flexibility the system may not be able to meet the needs of either the changing clergy or the changing laity whom it serves.

We know that changes within the gender, racial, and life-style mix have begun to alter the distribution of power within the church. We need to recognize that power shifts within any institutional structure always create tensions and stress. Nowhere does the church feel these tensions more acutely than within the appointment-making process.

Some bishops feel abused by clergy and laity who will not accept appointments. Some clergy spouses feel betrayed by cabinets whose decisions threaten to disrupt their career plans. Some Pastor-Parish Relations Committees of local churches feel mistreated by superintendents who seem more interested in placing available pastors than in addressing the needs of their particular church.

Nobody overtly regrets the disappearance of the "old boy" network. However, most of us were somewhat naive regarding the far reaching and unanticipated consequence of change. A major reason for the system's current dysfunctionality is the erosion of episcopal decision-making power. The more realistic the consultative process becomes, the more complicated appointment making will become. Some of us are apprehensive about the growing discontent and yearn for the days when clergy went where they were sent and congregations accepted their appointee without question. It was certainly an orderly system—somewhat repressive, but not as frustrating, complicated, and time-consuming.

Others believe that the pains we are experiencing are pains of rebirth. They are a sign that the church is alive in a pluralistic world and struggling to find new ways to respond. The urgent question is, can we make the itineracy flexible enough to accommodate the new voices adequately? Intuition tells me that if we do not make more changes, membership will continue to erode, and the church will fail to attract highly competent persons into the clergy role.

It is not productive to chastise any of the players in the process. However, the younger members of the conference are most frequently identified as the culprits. They are berated for their lack of commitment to the church when they refuse certain appointments. Undoubtedly there are some clergy who are selfish, lazy, or uncommitted. Many others are expressing legitimate concerns, standing up for what they believe to be right.

If we listen carefully to their concerns we may glean important clues about the ways in which the itineracy must be modified. The nonconforming clergy who assert themselves have much in common with the nonconforming laity, many of whom have left the church dissatisfied. We cannot ignore the concerns of either group. Enumeration of a few of these issues illustrates the need for a new response.

A Changing Cultural Ethic

Tex Sample describes a nearly 200-year history in which most Americans ascribed to an ethic of self-denial that has now been replaced with an ethic of self-fulfillment. He tells of a young woman who, when told that her ethic was selfish, replied, "Did Jesus not say, 'I came that you might have life and have it more abundantly'?"[6]

For many of the most gifted clergy born into the generation of self-fulfillment, this ethic involves giving their best in accordance with their talents. They also want to pay attention to the needs of their spouses and children. For example, if they are urban people trained in urban settings, they may resist being sent to rural parishes because they feel it is a waste of their talent and a burden on their families.

Scolding these persons is equivalent to blaming the victim, for example, blaming poverty on families who are caught in the welfare system. Systems analysis is our best first step toward adequate change.

The laity are also affected by the ethic of self-fulfillment. Young people often choose membership in large churches that offer good music, good church school programs, and good preaching in the style and theological tradition they espouse. When these young people attend a local church where a newly appointed clergyperson seems inappropriate to the needs of the congregation, the system will be judged incompetent. While some committed laypersons will stay to fight the system, others give up and go somewhere else.

Wade Roof and William McKinney assert that the realities of pluralism and privatism have done much to undermine traditional systems including the system of religious authority.[7] This distrust affects liberals and conservatives. It has produced a trend toward less centralized government and regulation, fostered the accountability movement in public education, truth-in-advertising campaigns, and other similar trends.

As trust in traditional authority figures erodes, other forms of authority gain allegiance. For example, in health care increasing numbers of persons are turning to nutritionists, physical therapists, and a proliferation of mental therapists. All of these caregivers are treating problems formerly treated by physicians, the traditional authorities in health care.

The erosion of traditional authority and the rise of new authorities is affecting religious practice as well. Mainline churches are losing members to the two fastest growing categories in the Princeton Religion Research Center's typology of religious preference, "unchurched" and "other." "Other" includes any religion that is not Catholic, Protestant, or Jewish; for example, Muslim, Buddhist, or New Age. Between the years 1952 and 1985 there was a 300 percent growth in the number of Americans checking "other" and a 350 percent growth in the number identified as "unchurched."[8] These figures should be heeded when we think about membership loss.

Even within the church the distrust of authority is growing. A recent book by lay leaders James W. Holsinger, Jr., and Evelyn Laycock addresses this issue. In their chapter titled "A Kept Clergy" they object to (1) the lack of ministerial competence and (2) the promotion mentality of appointment, alluding to the fact that seniority brings promotion, often without competence. The authors quote church critics Douglas Johnson and Alan Waltz, who discuss the widely held perception among clergy and laity that the appointment process is increasingly used to solve the organizational problems of the conference as a whole, and is not focused on serving the best interests of either the individual minister or the local church.[9]

This dissatisfaction encompasses both the "conservative" or evangelical laity and the "liberal" laity. It is present in all geographical areas. For example, Holsinger and Laycock are from the Southeastern Jurisdiction. A recent random survey of congregations in a Western Jurisdiction conference indicates the same kind of dissatisfaction. When asked, "How appropriate is your current pastoral appointment for the needs of your congregation?" 27 percent of the lay respondents deemed the current appointment inappropriate.[10]

How Shall We Interpret These Trends?

At this point some will jump from analysis to solution and suggest that the abolishment of the guaranteed appointment will solve the problem. I am not so sure. Before we move too quickly to a solution let us be sure that we (1) understand the causes of our problem clearly, (2) have it defined accurately, and (3) have gathered the right data on which to make a decision. Then we will be ready to experiment with some possible solutions. In today's political climate we should proceed cautiously when we advocate that the church abolish a system that protects the right of dissent within its clergy leadership. In the short run elimination of the guaranteed appointment may help cabinets weed out incompetent or unsuitable persons. In the long run the abolishment may lead to a repressive system in which socially active or nonconforming clergy can be dismissed for making the church uncomfortable with the status quo.

Changes in the Nature of Clergy Work

Analysis has convinced me that change in the nature of clergy work is the most important variable in the dysfunctionality of the itineracy. Much has been written recently that is critical of the way clergy approach their work. In that literature the difference between call and profession is frequently discussed. A common argument suggests that professionalization has secularized the ministry and created an atmosphere in which clergy are more concerned with salary and promotion than with being the servants of God. As Ross Kinsler explained, "Education for ministry used to be education for servanthood, now it has become education for privilege."[11]

Yet in *Contemporary Images of Christian Ministry,* Donald E. Messer reminds us that "originally, the concept of profession had a broad definition, roughly equivalent to a religious calling. . . . Professional work was a response to divine summons."[12] We are well served by this reminder of the original meaning of profession. Those of us who are lay professionals remind the clergy that responsible professionals, in medicine, law, teaching, or ministry, have historically viewed their work as a high calling. Furthermore, the most thoughtful members of each profession are just as worried about the increasing lack of commitment to calling as are the clergy.

To be reminded that the problem is not unique to the clergy is not to deny its seriousness. It does suggest that many of the same concerns exist in professions that do not have guaranteed appointments. It also indicates that the guaranteed appointment may be a symptom rather than the cause of our difficulty.

Another insight about clergy professionalism is illustrated by Messer with a quotation from Reinhold Niebuhr, who said as a young pastor in Detroit, "Sometimes when I compare myself with these efficient doctors and nurses hustling about I feel like an ancient medicine man dumped into the twentieth century." Messer goes on to observe that "seeking to overcome such feelings of impotence and powerlessness, a renewal of interest in the image of clergy as professionals has captured the thinking of many theological educators and pastors."[13]

Messer is suggesting that feelings of impotence and powerlessness preceded interest in professionalism, with a focus on higher salary and promotion. If this is true it may be more fruitful to look at clergy feelings of powerlessness than to focus on salary and promotion.

The secular sociologist Andrew Abbott provides a fresh approach to an analysis of the professional clergy. In his book, *The System of Professions: An Essay on the Division of Expert Labor,* he argues that the problem with most current analysis of professional behavior is that it focuses on structure rather than on work. He contends that it is more productive to focus on the ways that the link between a profession and its work are created in work rather than in structure.[14] Therefore, in tracing the development of the professional clergy he focuses on shifts in the nature of the work that clergy perform rather than on structural issues such as the process of appointment making.

Before the industrial revolution concern for personal salvation was a primary focus of clergy work. As the concern declined clergy filled the void by developing a growing concern for human problems in a changing society. (These included the upheavals caused by the industrial revolution as children went to work in factories, families were wrenched from the land, etc.) Clergy of the nineteenth century entered the fields of education and social melioration. At one point it was in those fields that they did most of their work.

The latter half of the twentieth century brought society's preoccupation with individual problems. Clergy responded by creating the pastoral care movement with emphasis on personal counseling as the work of the clergy.[15] If we accept Abbott's description we are led to an interesting question. What is the major work of the clergy today? What will it be in the twenty-first century? Until we can answer this question clearly and succinctly, the structure will be in disarray.

Abbott made another observation that can be useful to our discussion of the itineracy. He reminds us that when efficiency became a central value in the accomplishment of professional work, it brought increased bureaucracy to all professions, ministry included. In 1900 there were nine clergy for every one other person whose work focused on religious or psycho/social human concerns. In 1970 there was an even balance between clergy and kindred workers in these fields, for every one clergyperson there was one non-ordained person doing similar work.[16]

This proliferation of associated workers affects the appointive system. It can be a blessing to local church laity who need more staff but cannot afford to carry the burden of the ministerial benefit package for more than one or two clergy. It can be a problem for a system designed to place only ordained clergy into an area of work served by many other professionals or para-professionals.

Reshaping Our Vision of Ministry Must Precede Reshaping Our Structure

We are a society in which power is being redistributed and the nature of professional work roles is changing. These are but two of the factors that call for a reimaging of ministry. New approaches are being brought to the definition, some from feminist theologians. After affirming that we currently have no one, clear model of ministry, Rebecca Chopp observed recently that "professionalism is important in ministry, for it stresses the skills and competency of ministerial functions. But it is not a model of ministry based on any theological foundation."[17] As a layperson without formal training in theology I am unable to envision all that her statement implies.

One implication seems obvious. We must reexamine our attitude toward clergy compensation. Any creative new image of a flexible itineracy serving a multicultural world must be predicated on a revised remuneration system based on a more narrow range of salary differences. Too many of us, the generic church members, accept the secular world's measure of excellence—more money denotes better quality. Laity must bear a good deal of the responsibility for the undue interest in salary and promotion that is generally attributed to clergy. Congregations seem to be bidding for star pastors the way big league franchises bid on star ball players. That is dehumanizing for all of us, laity and clergy alike.

There are at least two precedents for equalization of salary that can serve as examples. In the school of medicine where I hold a faculty appointment, the physicians' private practice fees are pooled and then allocated first to the school of medicine for its needs and then to the doctors according to their productivity. A variation of that system could work for the church. Conferences could develop merit criteria that would define productivity in creative ways. A clergyperson along with her or his congregation might be rewarded for productivity in missional outreach to new populations or for the growth of cultural diversity within the congregation. Reward could still be defined as a higher salary for the clergyperson in that local church, but it would be based on concern for the needs of the connection as well as the needs of the local church.

We might also look at the clergy remuneration schemes of developing countries where the church is growing. For example, Mortimer Arias, former bishop of the Methodist Church of Bolivia, claims that in some parts of Latin America the youngest pastors are paid the highest salaries because they have young families to support![18] Does our astonishment at that idea stem from our theological understandings of ministry more than from our understanding of structure?

Lynn N. Rhodes, in her book *Co-Creating a Feminist Vision of Ministry,* suggests a model of ministry that is closely aligned with feminist theories. She speaks of "ministry organized contextually and defined by its vision." Its essential characteristics are (1) its mission is defined by discerning the church's understanding of how to incorporate its vision within specific historical contexts, and (2) its structural forms and leadership roles are designed to address the political, social, and religious needs of a particular situation.[19] I believe this vision holds promise.

Is it possible that lay dissatisfaction with incompetence and clergy frustration with impotence have occurred primarily because we have lost clarity of vision about the meaning of our theological commitment to ministry rather than because our structure is faulty? Is it possible that our denominational alienation from so many segments of contemporary society is because we, clergy and laity alike, need to reimage our theological commitment to the whole people of God?

Signs of Developing Adaptations

Earlier in the chapter it was suggested that recent structural adaptations provide insight into trends of the future. Other visionary insights may come out of a recent experiment that addressed the relationship between traditionally structured work roles and the need for more adequate response to the pains of the people. The assignment of Bishop Felton May to the drug crisis in Washington, D.C., attracted national attention. As the *New York Times* reported, "The church called on a never before used provision . . . in the *Book of Discipline* that permits the Council of Bishops to assign a member to a specific social issue for a period of up to two years."[20]

If we view that assignment from Abbott's sociological perspective it can be interpreted as a structural response that followed rather than preceded a concern about clergy work that was needed. The church was called to respond "where children deal drugs on urban streets where blight is the norm and rats as big as possums rummage garbage."[21] Viewed from Rhodes' theological perspective this is ministry in specific cultural context, shaped through the praxis of action and reflection.

Several concepts within this Council of Bishops' assignment may be useful in other settings: (1) The structural adaptation occurred because the church accepted responsibility for a population that was not being served adequately within the confines of traditional work patterns. (2) The people who need the ministry are not generic United Methodists. In all likelihood they will never become members of local churches as those churches are now structured. (3) The assignment was grounded in the work of local congregations. "I'm going to be the pastor's pastor. I will live with these pastors on a day-to-day basis, visiting the homes of the bereaved as well as working with those who have afflicted family members," said Bishop May.[22] (4) A person with special skills was needed for the job. Given the racial tensions and recent political events related to the drug crisis in Washington, D.C., it probably needed to be a high status, competent, respected, African-American man.

Newspapers all over the country found this appointment newsworthy.[23] Is that because they viewed it as a prophetic response to a needy world? Perhaps we should ask ourselves why such responses are not everyday occurrences in mainline churches. Is it naive to suggest that these conceptual elements become the basis of a new vision of the clergy role? Can Boards of Ordained Ministry give some attention to the special needs of their conference and seek to recruit candidates with special skills that address particular populations? Can seminaries and the Board of Higher Education and Ministry develop more continuing education courses for clergy whose assignments in our multicultural world require new skills? Can Councils of Ministry place renewed emphasis on the need for ministries outside the cultural framework of generic members like me?

If so, some new structural adaptations result. A bishop and cabinet might decide to develop some cluster profiles of different kinds of populations that need to be evangelized along with profiles of the types of clergy needed to start or revitalize churches in those neighborhoods. A Board of Ordained Ministry might put more emphasis on describing the particular needs of one or several parts of its Annual Conference as it interviews potential candidates. Persons could be recruited and/or reeducated based on their commitment to serve in these environments.

Such changes might incline an appointive cabinet to consult with conference members about the cultural contexts in which each feels that she or he could do the best job. Such observations could become part of the clergyperson's profile.

As a result of such re-visioning some local churches might broaden their concept of staffing. Members of high-steeple churches might decide to share a member of their larger staff with another local church or specialized ministry on a part-time or rotating basis in order to meet particular needs. The idea is not new. Church pairing is already in practice, and could be expanded in a variety of ways to enhance new ministries.

Such small changes could excite laity, particularly if the changes were part of the church's effort to provide competent leadership for relevant ministries. Clergy morale might be enhanced if individual clergy realized that they were not bogged down in structure, but that structure could actually empower them to use their special skills.

Vision, commitment, time, and patience on the part of all will be needed in order to develop workable solutions. If our own lost children, the poor and the homeless, the wounded and the hopeless are to know United Methodism and its ministers as servant-leaders[24] for Jesus Christ, we must not settle for structural alterations of the clergy itineracy system alone as the solution to our uncertainty about the mission of the church in a pluralistic world.

CHAPTER 8

Crossing Cultural, Racial, and Gender Boundaries

Susan M. Morrison and Gilbert H. Caldwell

The Opportunities Industrialization Center's (OIC) program was organized in Philadelphia by a Baptist clergyman, Leon Sullivan, and a United Methodist clergyman, Joshua Licorish. This worldwide program emphasized job training and preparation for persons who have historically been excluded from the job market. One slogan Sullivan popularized is a clear description of the program: "We screen people in rather than screen them out." It is our assumption that The United Methodist Church strives to be "barrier-free" in its mission and ministry. We, as a denomination, believe that we are called to "screen people in" in order for us to be faithful. We, therefore, share our concerns about, and commitment to, transcending cultural, racial, and gender boundaries.

Boundaries as Stepping Stones

Our experiences, respectively, as an Anglo-American woman and as an African-American man, have taught us that not every United Methodist layperson or clergyperson has been able to respond positively to the reality and subsequent mobility of clergy who are female and/or African, Asian, Latino, and Native American. We approach our topic with the hope that boundaries are beginning to become stepping stones, enabling God's diverse humanity to share, experience, interact, and practice a reciprocity that is living testimony to the power of what God has done in Christ.

Yet, we know boundaries have too often been erected to exclude rather than include. We write, not out of some distant observation of the exclusion of others, but rather out of our own firsthand experiences of exclusion. We have experienced the surprise, negativity, patronizing, stereotyping, evasiveness, and reluctance to cooperate by persons who find it difficult to affirm our humanity and/or acknowledge the validity of our calling. We have been in situations where persons through body language and hesitation express their uncertainty about our capacity to minister, share, and lead because we are female or a person of color.

Susan, who as a pastor, district superintendent, council director, and now a bishop, has encountered as a woman in ministry, hesitancy and uncertainty from some pastor-colleagues and laypersons, even though The United Methodist Church has ordained women since 1956.[1] Gilbert has experienced the surprise, reticence, and anger of clergy and laypersons as they have responded to his participation in the United Methodist itineracy. He remembers a family who stopped attending one church before his arrival because they could not accept a black pastor. When he visited them they could not admit the real reasons for their decision to cease participating in the church. All they could say was that "they finally realized they were Unitarian and not Methodist." He also remembers how one or two clergy in nearby churches eagerly provided alternative church participation possibilities for those families disgruntled over having a black pastor.

We suggest that a major limiting factor in church and society is the boundary of culture. Resistance to race and gender inclusiveness is taught and practiced in particular cultural perspectives. Culture is the collection of history, folkways, mores, assumptions, and practices of persons and groups. Sometimes our culture teaches us that certain persons "belong," while others do not. The "others" are excluded most often because members of the "in" group have had few, if any, close encounters with those who are different.

The challenge and opportunity for The United Methodist Church through its itinerant philosophy and appointive system is to create an alternative cultural system that counters prevailing systems that promote narrow homogeneity. The appointive system allows the denomination through the placement of clergy to broaden and deepen the cultural vision of churches and individuals.

appointment system anti-homogeneity

Facilitating Open Itineracy

Our experiences have taught us that it is possible to engage in effective ministry in those local churches that initially resisted our appointment. We have discovered that even those parishioners who were most reluctant to accept us because we were the "first" in time were able to respond to us as pastor, particularly in moments of personal and family crisis. We each can testify that when we were able to be present as pastor, friend, representative of the church, and spokesperson for the healing and liberating power of the faith, resistance was set aside and ministry took place.

To achieve open itineracy, we suggest the following ways to facilitate cross-racial appointments and the appointment of women. First, in The United Methodist Church it is imperative that persons who are subject to the appointive process, whether they are local pastors or ordained elders, be constantly reminded of our commitment to gender and racial inclusiveness in the denomination, and thus, also in the appointment-making process.

Second, it is essential that every United Methodist clergyperson understand that an important ingredient of ministry is the proclamation, teaching, and demonstration of the church's commitment to inclusiveness in every aspect of the work of the church. Apathetic and weak clergy leadership on issues of gender and race have given some United Methodists the assumption that Christian commitment in this arena is optional.

Third, staff-parish relations committees in every church must not only affirm this denominational commitment but share that commitment and understanding with the leadership and membership of the local church. A simple four-step process for individuals and churches to take leadership in undergirding and implementing open itineracy is as follows:

> (1) The identification, honestly and realistically, of our individual and group biases, and acceptance of traditions and practices of exclusion on racial and gender grounds. (2) Begin to imagine and experiment with new thoughts and practices, to challenge the attitudes and actions that have endorsed exclusion. (3) Develop new thought patterns and vocabulary that endorse, support, and affirm inclusiveness. (4) Practice, practice, practice! One of the many benefits of the development and practice of gender inclusive language is that we have had to think and internalize gender inclusiveness. Our goal is to shift from cultural practices that exclude, to inclusive cultural practices that affirm what we have believed as faithful United Methodists.

Fourth, if ministry is to be successful through our connectional policy, clergy and laity must acquire a renewed and deepened understanding of the work of appointment cabinets. The corporate nature of our ministry must be realized by all of us, particularly in the affirmation of itineracy and the making of appointments.

The Church as a Contrasting Community

The role of the church is to be a contrasting community. It is descriptive of a church unrestricted by the cultural captivity of the past. Our appointive system allows cabinets with vision, and the courage to enflesh the vision, an opportunity to demonstrate that effective ministry can occur through appointments that are cross-racial and in those that utilize the gifts of clergywomen.

Frederick Douglass, the abolitionist, understood that progress is the result of vision, courage, and a willingness to struggle. Douglass said that there are some persons who want rain without thunder and lightning, others want crops without plowing up the land, but if there is no struggle, there is no progress. This reluctance to struggle keeps us from crossing boundaries and exploring new territory. It robs us of the joy and satisfaction in challenging the status quo in faithfulness to God.

There are still individuals who have difficulty accepting the idea of women in ministry, particularly in pastoral leadership roles in the church. These persons offer a challenge to the leadership of the church. If church leaders do not want history to view them as perpetuators of a restrictive gender status quo, then leadership must be willing to criticize, confront, and transform the old assumptions. Theologian Rosemary Radford Ruether offers helpful counsel on this task:

> There are two ways to criticize things, an oppositional and a dialectical way. The oppositional way simply sets up an affirmation as a repudiation of its opposite. . . . I would regard my own mode of thinking as dialectical. I see negation, not as an attack on someone else's person or community, but as a self-criticism of the distortions of one's own being and community. Criticism of these distortions opens up the way for a positive reconstruction of the healing and liberating word of the tradition and capacities of human life. This is the healing and liberating word that I have heard emerge from the Christian tradition, once freed of its distorted consciousness.[2]

Those among us who are still uncertain and least committed to an open itineracy and an inclusive United Methodist Church must acknowledge that our proclamation and practice of the Christian gospel have been more consistent with the faith when we have been able to engage in a ministry of mission and evangelism, freed from the narrow exclusive restrictions of the past. Gender and racial exclusiveness are at variance with the United Methodist understanding of the Christian faith.

Sydney S. Sadio stresses the importance of open itineracy. Basing his thoughts on his experience as a black pastor of a predominantly white church in New Jersey, he writes:

> There will always be persons who will be prejudiced against black persons, and we have to admit that they are members of our churches. However, we cannot allow ourselves to be prevented from doing what we believe is the right thing simply to keep prejudiced persons in our congregations. . . . Even though black persons need positive black role models, it is just as important for white persons to have black role models and to experience blacks in leadership positions not only in the secular sphere but in local, predominantly white congregations. This will help to break down some of the stereotypical ideas which persons have about black pastors in particular.[3]

Sadio, a district superintendent in the Southern New Jersey Conference, is clear about the necessity of The United Methodist Church to be proactive in expressing its commitment to racial and gender inclusiveness. What he writes about race also is applicable to the appointment of women. The United Methodist Church, with its history of racial diversity and its commitment to ordain and appoint women, has an opportunity to witness to the world and a society that is still polarized. It can witness to a spiritual richness that results from the practice of authentic inclusiveness.

The Bugle of Leadership

Crossing longstanding cultural barriers requires courageous and farsighted leadership. Even in the church we know that we do not easily move from cultural mores to Christian practice. Martin Luther King, Jr., a keen observer of the church, raised the question: "Why is the church so often a taillight rather than a headlight?" King, with many others, reminded us that "eleven o'clock on Sunday morning is the most segregated hour in America."

We have assumed that major resistance to open itineracy is rooted within the attitudes of the laity. Clergy have sometimes used their assumptions about the "unreadiness" of laypersons to accept women or persons of color as pastors to justify moving slowly in the appointment process. In a 1983 research survey conducted to measure receptivity to open itineracy in the East Ohio Conference, laity support for appointments made by the cabinet was quite high.

We contend that race and gender are still considered barriers in the appointment process. Many clergy of The United Methodist Church have acquiesced to the restrictive racial and gender mores of the larger society. George E. Schreckengost, in an article entitled "The Effect of Latent Racist, Ethnic, and Sexual Biases on Placement," writes: "The most surprising discoveries in analyzing the data were the extent of laity support for appointments made by the cabinet and the low level of lay support estimated by the clergy."[4]

It is astounding that clergy who have participated in the appointment process as beneficiaries, and/or as those who make appointments, are sometimes less than supportive of "appointments made by the cabinet." This attitude diminishes our clergy deployment process as a vehicle for mission and evangelism.

We believe it is necessary for clergy to provide strong moral leadership if our denomination is to continue to be a major force for ministry in the 1990s and beyond. Donald E. Messer in *Contemporary Images of Christian Ministry* addresses the issue of leadership:

> The passivity of many Christian ministers, lay and clergy, ought to be a matter of concern. Many seem to expect to be told what to say and to think and how to act. . . . Persons who need outside permission for ministry are easily cowed by controversy and paralyzed by polarities of opinion. Those who spend all their time with their ears to the ground are in no position to move rapidly forward. One has to take responsibility for one's own life and ministry.[5]

The words of I Corinthians 14:8 are instructive at this point: "And if the bugle gives an indistinct sound, who will get ready for battle?" (NRSV). Ministers are expected to be buglers; it is essential to our calling.

Martin Luther King, Jr.'s "Letter from the Birmingham Jail" was addressed to clergy who in that tumultuous and tragic time failed to speak out against the injustices of segregation and to make efforts to correct them. The appointment process, the guaranteed appointment, and the commitment to inclusiveness of The United

Methodist Church are all dependent upon clergy who understand that they are called to leadership.

In her foreword to *Those Preachin' Women: Sermons by Black Women Preachers,* Prathia Hall Wynn of United Theological Seminary, writes:

> Although the tradition in which they stand has often been obscured by prejudice, it is, nevertheless, as old as Christian discipleship. Repeatedly, in defiance of the patriarchal exclusions of first-century culture, our Lord prepared women for ministry. Jesus welcomed women into his itinerant seminary, held high-level theological discussion about the nature of God and the character of true worship with a Samaritan woman at Jacob's well, commended Mary of Bethany for choosing to learn the truths of God at his feet, and transformed women mourners into women messengers at the site of the empty tomb. Commissioned by none other than the risen Christ, women first proclaimed the resurrection. Two thousand years later their daughters announce to disciples and to doubters, "We have seen the Lord." [6]

The church will always be peopled by disciples and doubters, but we must never allow the doubters to restrict or intimidate our commitment to practice open itineracy. Church leadership that is fearful of alienating those whose vision is limited to restrictive cultural patterns and practices aids and abets superficial ministry.

The United Methodist Church is in a unique position to offer leadership beyond our denominational boundaries. If we believe that God is calling us to cross all kinds of boundaries, then we must transcend our own boundaries. We call upon The United Methodist Church to enable every United Methodist local church to have firsthand experience of women in ministry, and the ministry of pastors of different racial identity and cultural background. This action will be a gift not only to ourselves, but also to the world. It can then be said of us as United Methodists, as was said in Joshua 6:20, "They gave a loud shout, and the walls collapsed."

CHAPTER 9

Conflicting Covenants: Clergy Spouses and Families

Bonnie J. Messer and Denise Johnson Stovall

The church was filled to capacity as a processional of United Methodist clergy crammed into the tiny sanctuary. It was an impressive sight in this small town to see so many of these ministers pay their respects to the fifty-year-old preacher, who had died of a heart attack just days before.

The congregation was impressed with the round of ministers who spoke, praising the pastor for giving all of his time to uplifting the church. In the eyes of his members, he was considered "a good minister" who never ignored the needs of the church. However, in the eyes of his family, he ignored their needs—and his own.

This exemplifies one dilemma facing clergy spouses and their families. In every regional area of the denomination, Annual Conference leaders can tell stories of clergy who worked hard for decades in local churches, on low salaries, and with minimum benefits for their families. Then, it all ended with a heart attack. The family was left to pay medical bills. They were forced to move from the parsonage and find housing. They became outsiders in a system that had determined their way of life—the itineracy.

Like all families, the clergy family is changing. Although not all of the tension experienced in the parsonage can be blamed on the itinerant system, it is important to consider whether the itineracy creates additional and undue stumbling blocks for ministerial families seeking to be faithful to the equally demanding commitments to the church and to the family.

Historical Perspective on the Role of the Clergy Spouse

In early Christendom, the norm was celibate clergy. Although Protestants have had married clergy for centuries, the image has persisted of clergy as persons who devote all of their time and energy to the church. Little recognition has been given to whether the minister fulfills his or her matrimonial vows. "Married to the church" is a frequent description of the clergy. John Wesley and Francis Asbury clearly preferred single clergy, free from what the 1844 General Conference referred to as "local embarrassments"—wives, children, and property.[1]

If the conditions experienced by early itinerant circuit riders discouraged the feasibility of marriage, so much the better. Frederick A. Norwood describes the itinerant preachers as "constantly on the go, exposed to all kinds of weather, especially vulnerable to epidemics and disease, for which, in addition to the expectancy of an eternal reward, they received less than $100 per year."[2] These single young men were promised nothing when they entered the traveling ministry or when they retired from it. "They were nevertheless expected to give all of themselves to their calling. And they did, by the hundreds, worn out before they were forty."[3] Although the expectations of the itinerant minister have changed in many ways over the years, the underlying model of itineracy for many people continues to be that of young, single men entering into a covenant that requires unquestioning self-sacrifice on the part of the preacher.

As the church pushed into new frontiers, more and more Methodist clergy married. A home and family helped offset some of the burdens of the itinerant's meager life-style; however, it also added new stresses. Mary Orne Tucker's autobiography of life as an itinerant preacher's wife in the early 1800s described her discomfort upon realizing that she had only one cup of flour and one potato left in the house and no indication of when her husband would return.[4] Appointed to a different circuit every year, one could never be sure what arrangements had been made for housing or financial remuneration. Mrs. Tucker described her family, which included four young children, being sent to a community that was in dire financial straits. She commented, "What motive influenced our presiding elder to recommend this station to the Conference for Mr. Tucker . . . was a mystery to us; but to stay was impossible, and we had no alternative but to throw ourselves and helpless children upon our friends for present support."[5]

Herrick M. Eaton, writing in 1851, observed that the itinerant's wife must "endure the hardships and privations of the poor, but is denied their exemptions and immunities."[6] Unfortunately, some clergy families can echo these concerns today as they are appointed to churches that are unable to pay the pastor's salary regularly and allow pension benefits to be significantly in arrears. The church's unwillingness to ensure adequate salaries for clergy families has resulted in many spouses seeking employment outside the home to bring the family out of genteel poverty.

In the past, the clergy family revolved around the ordained parent's role.[7] These were one-income households in which the husband earned a wage (meager though it might be), and the wife was expected to care for the household and the children and to participate in a supportive manner in all aspects of her husband's ministry.

In the early Protestant church, no one discussed a role for the minister's wife outside the manse, and no one thought of a spouse who was not female. For women not married to clergy, their contribution to the growing church was recognized only minimally. Although they housed and fed the itinerant minister, opened their homes for Bible study and prayer meetings, and provided models of a devoted Christian life-style they were not regarded as church leaders. Throughout most of Protestant history, women could not become pastors in their own right. Thus, to be in active ministry, women had to marry clergy. This reality has changed.

Recognition of the divergent models chosen by clergy spouses has increased in the latter part of the twentieth century. William Douglas's 1965 study, one of the first to delineate clearly more than the traditional role for the minister's spouse, identified the "teamworker," the "background supporter," and the "detached."[8] Since the 1960s, the images have multiplied dramatically: clergy married to clergy, women pastors with spouses, and clergy and spouses living in separate cities.

Male spouses of clergy have helped highlight the insensitivity of the itinerant system to the needs of female spouses and children.[9] They have modeled alternative responses to expectations by the minister and the church that the main responsibility of the clergyperson's spouse is to serve the church. Male spouses report that the church is frequently quite understanding of their conflicting schedules and does not expect them to participate in every church activity. Clergy spouses, both male and female, have joined in a chorus advocating consideration of the needs of all family members.

A New Understanding of Vocation

G. Lloyd Rediger in "Revolution in the Parsonage" advocates a new understanding of vocation, in which "vocation applies to each individual, without theological priority."[10] He affirms that it is "theologically sound to say a pastor's calling is not only to the church, but also to his or her marriage, family and self." Recognizing that we are in a time of transition, Rediger states that we can "no longer pretend that the status quo is adequate. We need to open the door to new options that allow everyone to live more freely and faithfully." The United Methodist Church must respond to this mandate if it is to be seen as a viable vocational option for persons who affirm the needs of all family members.

Arbitrary episcopal appointments can be very destructive of marital and family life. For many clergy spouses, the requirement to itinerate presents a major obstacle that interferes with the further development of their own careers. School teachers and librarians can lose tenure, prized teaching assignments, and retirement benefits. A specialized lawyer in international trade cannot relocate to a rural area and expect to find a position. A research scientist needs access to her or his specialized equipment as well as the support of trained colleagues. A tenured university professor of classical music cannot quickly find an equivalent teaching position. Physicians and psychologists spend years building practices that cannot be easily replicated in a new community.

A frequently ignored group is the people who never complete seminary or who complete seminary but choose not to take the vows of ordination. One reported reason for not completing the process of ordination is the anticipated conflict between the pledge to itinerate and the marital vows which pledge one to consider the needs of one's mate. How strictly the bishop and cabinet apply the requirement to itinerate varies from conference to conference. In some conferences, clergy report that the cabinet seeks to take into consideration the needs of the family (for example, the Memphis Conference Studies found that 86 percent of those surveyed believed that the appointment system gave some consideration to the spouse's occupation).[11] In other conferences clergy are frequently moved in response to arbitrary standards such as the number of years one has served in a particular parish or the need to change all pastors when the senior pastor moves. The primary concern is that the itineracy gives pastors and their families a sense that they lack control over very basic aspects of their lives.

Psychological Implications of Itineracy

Discussions of the tribulations experienced by clergy families usually highlight the profound loneliness they feel. A survey of United Methodist clergy families in Kansas found that clergy and spouses reported that they did not have close friends in their church or community.[12] Although clergy in all denominations acknowledge being set apart by members of their communities, frequent moves add to the itinerant family's isolation. Community persons hesitate to make the investment involved in developing meaningful relationships with the itinerant clergy family, who they view as "temporary" residents.

In advising the itinerant's wife in 1851, the Reverend Eaton warned that she could expect her life to be a "series of goodbyes." He described the pastor's wife as a "pilgrim and a stranger, having no continuing city from the time she leaves her paternal abode till she enters upon her final rest."[13] The lack of affirmation and the loneliness encountered by the uprooted spouse and family continues to be a problem in contemporary clergy homes.

Audrey T. McCollum in *The Trauma of Moving* asserted that there is a "price" in relocating. Persons experience a loss of identity, depression, and feelings of worthlessness. "The price is all the harder to pay because it goes unrecognized and unnamed."[14] Not only does one deal with the trauma of the present move, but unresolved issues from previous moves also resurface.

Positive adjustment to a move requires that a person exercise a sense of choice with insight and concern for self as well as others. An arbitrary implementation of the itinerant system can result in an appointment in which the pastor and family feel that they have no choice.

Historically, spouses have submerged their needs and sought to abide with what was interpreted as being in the best interests of the clergy and the church. Certainly, the denomination has discouraged the development of reflective choice making on the part of women or men if it interfered with the appointive powers of the church's hierarchy. Nevertheless, the human cost to the persons whose needs have been ignored in the equation has been high.

Scholars have documented the relationship between loss of a sense of control, decreased self-esteem, and increased depression.[15] McCollum speaks of a "loss of self." In other words, moving can cause a person to feel like "a nobody" and to experience "psychological annihilation."[16]

The importance of autonomy, or a sense of choice, is very clear. Under the itinerant system, the bishop still reserves or retains the final word in whether and/or where a person moves. In the 1988 Episcopal Address, the bishops told clergy and spouses that "the minister who places personal and unofficial limits on itineracy can have no assurance of such limits being honored nor appointment within such limits guaranteed."[17] Excessive authoritarianism can be personally devastating.

Ruth in the Old Testament exemplifies an ancient image of commitment frequently applied to the clergy family. She said to her mother-in-law, "Whither thou goest, I will go" (Ruth 1:16 KJV). Ruth surrenders unconditionally to her husband's family. Like Ruth, the minister's spouse has been expected to willingly say, "Whither thou goest. . . ." However, clergy spouses must be able to consider their needs and those of their families if they are to respond freely to the calling of the church.

Contemporary Images of Spouses

Being a clergy spouse is no longer the primary source of identity for most spouses. While the spouse's involvement in the church may still remain significant, he or she possesses a clearer sense of his or her own identity.

Persons who have provided models for contemporary clergy spouses include Leontine Kelly, who continued her education after raising her children and was elected the United Methodist bishop for the San Francisco area; Natalie Sleeth, a distinguished composer of sacred music; Neil Fisher, president of Garrett-Evangelical Theological Seminary, whose wife, Ila, presently serves as a pastor in suburban Chicago; Laura Deming, editor of SPICE (a clergy family publication), a cellist with the Lyric Opera of Chicago half the year and whose husband is a pastor in Michigan; Cynthia Wilson-Felder, a diaconal minister and minister of music who led worship services for the United Methodist Women's Assembly in 1986 and The Gathering in 1990; Raquel Martinez, a member of the board of directors for the

General Board of Global Ministries' Women's Division, who is minister of music at Emanu-El United Methodist Church where her husband serves as pastor; Mark Toner, a dedicated layman and father who works for Denver's Transportation Department and whose wife, Cynthia, returned to seminary while they cared for five children at home. All of these persons contribute to the kaleidoscope of images of persons married to clergy.

Conflicting Covenants

The itineracy poses a plethora of conflicts for the clergyperson who seeks to combine an active, vital ministry with the responsibilities involved in marriage and parenthood. An inevitable tension exists between the vows of ordained ministry and the marriage vows. However, the itineracy increases the tension by insisting that clergy, and hence their families, itinerate at the pleasure of the bishop and cabinet. Consideration of the needs of the family (employment, schools, emotional well-being) varies widely from conference to conference.

In exploring the dilemmas posed for the committed United Methodist clergy and their families, it is imperative that several underlying assumptions and values be considered. The nature of the covenant of ordination and the covenant of marriage need examination. Too often the church focuses only on the covenant of ordination to the exclusion of the marital covenant. If the church honestly champions marriage and the family in our society, then it dare not contradict what it preaches for laity by advocating less for its clergy.

John F. Childress and John Macquarrie in *The Westminster Dictionary of Christian Ethics* point out that covenants have been seen historically as agreements between unequals.[18] The Old Testament covenants existed between God and the people, though they were initiated by God, not negotiated. The covenants expressed God's power and grace. God expected the people to respond in grateful obedience.

The vows taken by persons seeking to be circuit riders in the early Methodist Church exemplified unequal covenants. While the expectations of the itinerant minister have changed in many ways over the years, the vows of ordination continue to be an expression of obedience on the part of the clergy to the episcopal leadership of the church.

Since its advent, itineracy assumed a hierarchy of priorities to which any "true believer" agreed to adhere. One's loyalties are first to God and the church, followed in order of decreasing importance by one's local congregation, the needs of individual families within the congregation, the pastor's needs, the spouse's needs, and finally, one's family. Actually, the needs of the spouse and family generally have not been clearly considered or have been ignored, as were the minister's needs. The family's primary mission was to enhance the growth and life of the church. One spouse described her struggles in an unsightly parsonage. When the district superintendent came for a visit, she was pleased to have him ask her directly how things were going *for her*. She naively believed he was interested and shared with him some of her concerns. When she finished, the superintendent did not blink an eye, but thanked her for lunch and quickly departed without any response. Needless to say, the wife felt very devalued.

Clergy, spouses, and their families are challenging the *prima facie* prioritizing of the vows of ordination. There are two important covenants into which a clergyperson has voluntarily entered and which must be honored by clergy, the local congregation, and the leadership of The United Methodist Church.

Although persons voluntarily enter into both the vows of ordination and the vows of matrimony, the covenant of marriage represents a covenant of equals in which two persons seek to join their lives in *mutual* affirmation and commitment. In marriage, "separate individuality is not destroyed but enhanced."[19] The emphasis centers on mutual acceptance and enduring responsibility. Rather than a covenant that stresses unequal obligations, the focus is on a caring relationship.

Patriarchal societies created hierarchies in which women and children and their needs had lower status, but these outdated images offer little insight into how concerned Christians can sort out conflicting demands between the church and the family in the 1990s. A more relevant model of covenant for the church and its clergy would provide for a mutuality of commitments. While the clergy need to be concerned about what is best for the church, the denomination must demonstrate clearly its concern and commitment to the best interests of ordained ministers and their families.

Ethical Considerations

In re-examining the itinerant form of ministry, one needs to consider some ethical implications. The ethical principles of autonomy and fidelity provide important guidelines in responding to the requirements of itineracy. The itinerant system interferes with the *autonomy* of the minister's family; that is, the freedom to make decisions about one's own life and to act on them, as long as they do not interfere with the rights of others. Autonomy is a process in which the needs of all those involved are considered. While the pastor has autonomously chosen to enter into ordained ministry and thus to abide by the cabinet's decisions, the minister's spouse and children may not feel that they have had equal input in the decision-making process, which directly affects their lives.

Clergy families are frequently expected to move when it is not optimal. Children are forced to leave friends; their education is disrupted. Examples include expectations to move before a teenager's final year in high school or in the middle of a school year or when a student has just been selected for participation in a competitive sport or activity at school or leaving an educational system with special academic support systems for a community with limited resources. While the pastor can usually anticipate new challenges and a welcoming congregation, the spouse may face the dilemma of leaving friends, a supportive environment, a cherished home, and a challenging job with no promise of equivalent employment. Bureaucratic decisions that provide for little autonomy frequently result in great emotional turmoil and pain for individual family members.

Many students in seminary are second-career persons who enter seminary with families who did not anticipate that a mate or parent would respond to the call of ministry. While the student excitedly attends classes on biblical criticism or feminist theology, the spouse seeks to cope with a miniature kitchen, a communal laundry in the basement, teenagers cramped into a single bedroom, and the necessity of finding a job with few prospects for anything much above minimum wage.

A second ethical guideline that needs to be considered is *fidelity.* Marriage is a fiduciary relationship. The couple promises loyalty and faithfulness to each other, with a clear expectation, a trust, that each person will be concerned about the best interest of the other. Margaret A. Farley, in *Making, Keeping, and Breaking Personal Commitments* suggests that we should not need to be vigilant in a love relationship. Rather, we should be able to "let go" and trust that we are loved. However, she cautions against foolish patience which tolerates injustices.[20] Can the itinerant system be trusted, or does the minister need to be on guard so that the itinerant system does not interfere with a mate's commitment to be caring? Are clergy encouraged or coerced to ignore the needs of their mates or children in the process of honoring their commitment to the church?

Farley illustrates the dilemma of conflicting claims through a personal example. In choosing between honoring her promise to go to her daughter's rehearsal and helping a client who had a fire, she suggests one needs to consider the larger context. How often does this come up? Is this client always in crisis? Does she usually make her daughter's rehearsals, or is there always some other higher priority? Families soon learn whether they can *trust* the clergy parent to honor commitments to the family and its needs.

Clergy families have a right to expect that their lives will not be harmed in the process of serving a congregation. Their needs are too frequently sacrificed for the needs of the church or of individual church members. While emergencies need to be accommodated, the minister's family need to know that they too, are important and not always the lowest priority. Self-esteem is not fostered in a home where one's needs are consistently ignored. In an age when the family faces many challenges, clergy families should be able to affirm and model the importance of each family member.

Dilemmas Demanding Attention

In reforming itineracy, special attention to the dilemma of clergy spouses and families is imperative. What follows are illustrative examples of areas in which the churches need to be more sensitive to the needs of the spouse and family.

First, clergy should be given larger salaries and be assured of better benefits. Historically, the clergyperson had not been well paid, but this was offset by the wide respect the clergy enjoyed within the community. If the local pastor is similar to other professionals or a chief executive officer of a company, his or her family should be compensated for the hours they all sacrifice for the service rendered to the institution. One local minister's wife said, "Sometimes it's degrading for me to see the way my husband works in the local church, because he knows he is not being treated fairly by the members. At times he is not paid a full salary, and he has not had his pension paid in months. Yet the members want us to dress nicely and portray the image of a well-to-do, middle-class family. With this present system, we can't do it."

Second, members of local churches must realize that the treatment of clergy in this decade will determine whether our youth accept the call to join The United Methodist Church. One pastor's spouse declared, "Our local churches need to educate the members on how to minister to the minister and the minister's family. What are we saying indirectly to the children of our pastors if we don't encourage the parent to respond to the children's needs?" She added that "congregations can make or break a minister," which may cause the clergyperson to neglect his or her health and to age too quickly.

Third, congregations must recognize that clergy families are also human, and experience the same crisis situations as the lay members. One clergy spouse lamented, "The problem is, they can get in trouble and want our help, but if we get in trouble, we are expected to help ourselves." She added that this is especially true in problems with children. "The pastor's children are expected to be angels, but they are just like other children." As another example, an urban minister struggled with his son's drug addiction. He told a United Methodist group that he was so busy helping the neighborhood youth in crisis that he never knew his own son was hooked on cocaine. Today, he advocates The United Methodist Church provide support systems to clergy families with addicted family members.

Fourth, the old adage "a home is a person's castle" may not be true for the local pastor and needs to be respected. If the clergy family live in a parsonage, the congregation determines if the family is comfortable or miserable. One preacher told the story of conflict in his family when he could not convince the church trustees to make repairs on the parsonage furnace. His wife and children almost became ill when the temperature dropped one night and the house had no heat.

In recent years, it must be said that district superintendents have worked diligently with Pastor-Parish Relations Committees to ensure that parsonages are in proper condition. But congregations do not understand that maintaining a good parsonage helps to maintain good relations with and within the parsonage family.

Another issue is the attitude of some congregations that the family should feel grateful to have a home. One clergy spouse remarked that "after encountering that attitude over the years, my husband and I decided to purchase our home. Members seem to treat you better when they know that you are not dependent on them for a roof over your head."

Fifth, the expectations imposed on clergy spouses by the Annual Conference, district, and local church should "change with the times." Many spouses, who were informally interviewed by the authors, agreed that the church still views them as "the church hostess" or "unpaid help." In some ethnic churches, this notion is especially true, for instance, when the spouse is asked to feed and house guest ministers for revivals and homecomings on the family's household budget.

Sixth, greater sensitivity to some of the newer dimensions of the itinerant system, such as two-career families and men married to clergy, must be accorded. In the study "Men Married to Ministers," Laura Deming and Jack Stubbs conclude that "the struggle is of prime importance to the church. The religious understanding of the ordained ministry 'to set apart' implies the importance in which ministry has been held historically." The "spiritual call" brings a different dimension to ministry and marriage than to other two-career marriages.[21] The calling was and is sacred. Often, what was sacrificed was the family, spouse, and the spouse's career, concluded Deming and Stubbs.

If this belief still holds true in The United Methodist Church, the question for the itinerant system of the future is "What are the implications for the increase of male clergy spouses?" Will the husband be expected to be mobile in the early stages of the wife's ministerial career? Will the Annual Conference understand the husband not surrendering a professional job that gives him respect and a high salary (sometimes better than his ordained wife)? Or will the clergywoman's career be considered "secondary" to her husband's profession? Will she be taken seriously by the local church if she changes congregations based on her husband's promotions?

Beyond Utilitarianism

For too long the church's paternalistic motivations have been assumed to be benevolent. Autonomous thinking was discouraged. The church has been given the benefit of the doubt that it would obviously do what was best for clergy and their families. Many question whether itineracy is not a utilitarian concept that places the good of the larger church over the good of its individual members, in particular, the families of clergy. The itineracy assumes that the bishop and cabinet know better than the clergy and their spouses what is needed. A self-centered focus that looks only at the interests of the individual is not an acceptable alternative. Rather, the church needs to find a more equitable balance between the needs of the institutional church and the clergy families who faithfully serve it.

CHAPTER 10

Married to the Church and to Each Other: Clergy Couples

Kenneth L. Waters and Lydia J. Waters

Are clergy couples a promise or a problem for the itineracy system? Undoubtedly, clergy couples are a phenomenon never envisioned or anticipated by John Wesley, Francis Asbury, and other architects of our method of ministerial deployment. If, however, in some proleptic moment, they had seen the possibilities of two clergy married to each other, there would still be the question of whether they would have received these possibilities as a potential blessing to the church or shunned them as an ominous bane to the appointment process.

What Wesley or Asbury would do is not as crucial as what we do in the context of our contemporary experiences. First, we are compelled, probably by our preacher's hearts, to affirm a biblical precedent for our experiences in the witness and ministry of Priscilla and Aquila (Acts 18:2, 18-26; Rom. 16:3-4), evangelist companions of Paul the Apostle, who are the earliest known prototypes of the clergy couple. Perhaps they show that from the beginning, clergy couples are an inevitable occurrence in the Christian ministry. Whether they are an inevitable help or hindrance is the question we seek to explore.

We Have Insights to Share

The emergence of clergy couples within The United Methodist Church has generated a peculiar set of issues, the very existence of which requires reasoned responses from clergy couples themselves. While there is no denying that bishops, district superintendents, other clergy and their spouses, and laity are able to empathize to some extent with the unique problems of clergy couples, their capacity for empathy can be strengthened by insights shared from within the special circumstances of clergy couples.

A clergy couple, of course, is a man and a woman, each of whom is an ordained, itinerating minister, who are married to each other. There may be some justification for applying the label to couples where at least one of the partners is a licensed local pastor or diaconal minister. After all, there are for the most part few conspicuous differences between the way that they and an ordained couple might function in a parish or other assignment. This, however, can only be done by using the term *clergy* loosely, by disregarding the technical meaning of *clergy* as "ordained persons." According to paragraphs 309.1, 406.1, and related portions of the 1988 *Discipline,* licensed local pastors and diaconal ministers are still laypersons. A particular constraint for us as authors is imposed by our concern for the implications of itineracy and related matters for clergy who are married to each other. Only ordained deacons and elders are claimed by the itineracy in The United Methodist Church. Nevertheless, licensed local pastors and diaconal ministers are ministerial specialists who are usually included in the embrace of clergy collegiality. When they are married to ordained persons or even to other local pastors or diaconals they are usually received as clergy couples, notwithstanding the restricting definitions of disciplinary language.

Reportedly, there are 778 clergy couples in The United Methodist Church. That is 1,556 constituent clergy couple members. These numbers, which have been determined from figures submitted by conference offices, are not categorically precise.[1] They include unordained persons like local pastors. Still, even with a smaller figure reflecting only ordained persons we would have a number too large to ignore, but yet not large enough to elicit unsolicited consideration of their special circumstance.

Therefore, the challenge of clergy couples is to achieve a fair balance between their needs and concerns and those of the greater church, to demonstrate how consideration of clergy couples and their families intersect with the good of the denominational family, and to preserve the fragile bases for sound marriages, nurtured family lives, and fruitful ministries.

So Are We a Problem or What?

The issues generated by the phenomenon of clergy couples are multiplex. Is the presence of clergy couples a promise of vital ministries or a burden upon the itineracy system? Is special consideration for clergy couples a fair request or an imposition upon the appointment process? Shall the primary criterion for clergy couple appointments be competence for ministry or what the cabinet has available "at the end of the day"? What preparation is needed in congregations receiving one or both members of a clergy couple? What housing provisions are called for by the unique situations of clergy couples? What is fair in regard to salary and benefit packages for the partners in a clergy couple? Has enough been done to ensure adequate health insurance for clergy couple families as well as adequate pension credit toward retirement? How does a clergy couple develop a proper balance between the doubled demands of the church and the demands of family and the marriage itself? What is expedient when a clergy couple, though compatible as husband and wife, proves incompatible as a ministry team? What is expedient when the otherwise proficient ministry of one partner is compromised by the inefficiency of the other? How should the conference and local church respond to the dissolution or breakdown of a clergy couple marriage? What sociological and cultural realities should be taken into account in the deployment of clergy couples?

The weight and multiplicity of these issues may be enough to justify the charge of the former district superintendent, whom we heard on more than one occasion say, "Clergy couples are a problem." We took the remarks in stride, but still they force our initial question whether clergy couples are a promise of vital ministry or a problem for the itinerate system.

The perception of clergy couples as a problem seems to begin with a couple's request that they be appointed at close proximity to each other if the assignments are separate or, if assigned together, to a congregation able to sustain both of them with amenities commensurate to the rank and training of each. In the former case, fulfilling the request may require that one or more vacancies be created in order to place each member of the couple. Ideally, the creation of such vacancies will be justifiable and acceptable to all parties involved, especially to the clergy who are vacated and probably reassigned elsewhere. The problem ensues to the degree that satisfaction with the appointments falls short of the ideal. In the latter case, satisfying the request may require assignment to one of the stronger, more firmly established congregations in the conference; the kind usually reserved for "seasoned" and "tenured" clergy. Depending on the "ethos" of the conference, particularly as it relates to the appointment process, this may be a barrier for clergy couples with relatively few years' experience in the ordained ministry.

There is also the matter of matching clergy with "compatible" congregations. The question of compatibility must be asked for all clergy appointments, but when the question must be asked of two members of the same family the answer may be complicated by logistics. What if after an appointment is determined for one clergy partner, there are no compatible appointments in the same area for the other partner? We have seen the kind of difficulty that occurs, for example, when a pastor at one end of the "liturgical-evangelical" worship spectrum is assigned to a congregation that is, for the most part, at the other end of the spectrum, or when a pastor at one end of the "liberal-conservative" theological continuum is assigned to a membership that is, for the most part, at the other end.

When all is said and done, clergy couples hope for an arrangement that will allow the coexistence of a sound marriage with strong ministries. If hope turns to hardship, it may be because the itineracy system itself is built around the model of the "traditional" clergy family wherein only one member of the family—namely, the husband—is clergy and the wife is unemployed except as a support for her husband and the various activities of "his" church. Should this be the case, then clergy couples are not the only challenge to the system. Clergy married to lay spouses with career-track professions are also a problem, especially if spouses are tied by their jobs to a specific locale or if the possibility of career advancement calls for relocation to a place distant to their mates' ministerial assignments. Clergy couples are unique in this context only because both partners are claimed by and have a claim upon the itinerate system.

Let's Weigh Our Options

Three basic options appear available to the itinerating network in regard to clergy couples. Clergy couples can make unusual personal sacrifices to adjust to the itinerate system; clergy couples can resign themselves to some third- or fourth-rate status within the system; or the itinerate system itself could be made to change or evolve until it is more compatible with contemporary clergy lives. We could argue that holding to the first and second options would soon have an eviscerating effect upon clergy couples, not to mention the ministry as a whole.

It is more within the economy of this discussion to contend that the United Methodist ministry itself and the church as a result faces slow evisceration if the third option is not pursued. One proposal is that equitable salary and other conference funds be deployed to help weaker congregations sustain a clergy couple, with the expectation, of course, that the congregation would in time become able to wean away from outside support. There are clergy couples who work extremely well together. Their conjoined ministries would offer the promise of renewal and revitalization for a struggling congregation.

Nevertheless, the vision and priorities of the itineracy network are such that the promise of clergy couples is often overlooked and funds are not set aside to enable their ministries. Our proposal would eliminate much of the need for creating vacancies for the sake of clergy couple appointments. Pulpit vacancies occur in natural course through promotion, demotion, request for transfer, sickness, retirement, and death. When an opening naturally occurs clergy couples can be appointed and the means provided to sustain their appointment. We realize that the idea of "naturally occurring vacancies" may be suspect from the perspective of someone who is reassigned or unassigned against his or her wishes, but no one needs to be forced out just to make room for a clergy couple.[2] Should the occasion arise for a clergy couple to be reassigned to a larger work or to separate but nearby parishes, this can happen as part of the natural course of cabinet decision making.

We served together in the same congregation during our first year in our present conference, even though Kenneth was the one who was actually appointed to the church. We both had several years of pastoral experience in separate assignments in the state where we previously lived. We struggled along on Kenneth's salary during our first year since our hopes for Lydia's appointment did not materialize. Limited funds were made available by the conference to support a "program director" at the church, and so we took advantage of that for Lydia. Despite the economic difficulties we had a blessed ministry through this congregation.

The model of a husband and wife clergy team seemed especially attractive to young adult married couples in our congregation and community. The church experienced renewal and growth primarily through the influx of young adult couples. After a year, Lydia was appointed to a separate congregation in the same city. Her appointment occurred as a natural result of her predecessor's retiring and members of that church requesting her. We experienced our separation as a mutual loss, but we knew that this was a wonderful opportunity for Lydia. Kenneth remained in this first appointment for two more years. Since our churches were close together, these two years were characterized by an unprecedented high degree of fellowship and cooperation between the two churches.

These two years were also periods of rapid growth for the two congregations due largely to the influx and interchange of young adults. Nevertheless, there are problems that come with church growth. One problem occurs when church members feel threatened by the appearance of new faces, and cabinet representatives fail to understand the dynamics involved. Kenneth was reassigned to a church in a nearby city and different district. After two more years Kenneth was appointed to a larger responsibility. Lydia has remained in her appointment which has doubled in membership over the past several years. Because of the distance between our churches, it is a little more difficult to achieve the kind of intercongregational fellowship that we saw before, but we are making good progress. Our experience has shown us that clergy couples need not be a problem. Whether serving one, two, or more congregations, whether serving together or separately, the leadership of a clergy couple can be a source of renewal and vitality for the church of Jesus Christ.

What's Fair Is Fair

Is special consideration for clergy couples a fair request or not? It is a fair request unless there is some qualitative difference between special consideration for clergy couples and that for, say, a clergy family where the lay spouse is a career-track professional or the children are at critical stages in their school experience. Comparisons can also be made to special requests on the basis of temporary or chronic health problems, ethnic identity, language skills or deficiencies, worship style, theological attitudes, time and tenure in ministry, or even aspirations for episcopal office. Since we are unconvinced of any qualitative difference between the kinds of requests that clergy couples make and those others make, then we must claim that our requests are also fair.

It could be claimed that all special requests are an unfair imposition upon the appointment process. Such a claim would ineluctably presuppose the continued validity and relevance of the traditional clergy family model, a model that poses few problems for the itineracy system if any at all. We would argue, however, that the pool of traditional clergy families has rapidly diminished, and for this reason any claims presupposing that model are quite untenable.

Requests for special consideration in the appointment process are a matter of course. They demonstrate the richness of experience within the coterie of clergy families. This range of experience can be a valuable resource for the church, which must minister to individuals and communities of varied backgrounds. The difficulties involved in meeting special requests including those of clergy couples can be balanced by the potential for good in particular appointments. Everyone will not be satisfied all the time, nor is this possible, but the attitude with which cabinets handle special requests can help make the postponement of desired situations more bearable.

We submit that, given our contemporary situation, it is not appropriate to say, "Clergy are here to serve the itineracy and not vice-versa." The itineracy system and the clergy are here to serve each other. They, in fact, need each other and for both to benefit there must be a fair degree of give-and-take. Therefore, when a clergy couple requests appointments to separate but neighboring congregations, their wishes need not be considered an imposition upon the labors of the cabinet but as an opportunity for fruitful ministries.

We are advocating a shift in attitude. We do so while acknowledging that not all bishops, district superintendents, clergy, and laity are in need of an attitude change insofar as there is ample evidence of sensitivity toward clergy couple concerns. We also do not pretend to know what goes on inside the closed quarters of a cabinet meeting, since neither one of us has been a district superintendent or bishop. We only know that there have been times when clergy couples have believed that their appointments were meted out on the basis of what was "left over" rather than upon their experience and ability, and that their treatment has indicated prior relegation to some unacknowledged category of "problem appointments." When clergy couples are viewed as a promise rather than a problem, then the potentiality of their appointments becomes more prominent in discussion than the difficulties they pose. Clergy couples would at least be assured that their gifts and graces for ministry were highlighted early in the appointment process, if for no other reason than the affirming nature of their involvement in the consultation aspect of appointment making.

We Need Advocacy

Beyond the walls of the cabinet meeting room, where most of us live or at least survive, there is the question of how local churches should prepare for the appointment of one or both members of a clergy couple. The advocacy of the district superintendent is of pivotal importance, particularly in interpreting the new situation to a congregation that has never been intimately involved with a clergy couple. Ideally, the church would be prepared to see a radical departure from anything even approximating the traditional clergy family model. If the couple is to be serving together, the church would need to be sensitized to the role of each member of the team as an ordained professional and pastor. If the couple is to be separate, their respective congregations may need help in reconciling themselves to the absence of the pastor's spouse.

Among the areas most critically in need of the superintendent's supervision is that of ministerial compensation and its various components, not the least of which is housing. It would be difficult to avoid fueling a controversy at this point. We have already done so by alluding to housing as compensation. According to paragraph 256.3f of the 1988 *Discipline,* "Housing shall not be considered as part of compensation or remuneration, but shall be considered as a means provided by the local church, and for the convenience of the local church, to enable its ministry and the itinerant ministry of the Annual Conference." This statute has been strenuously challenged by clergy couples since its inception in 1984. The housing issue is complex, and is not without its subtleties.[3]

Unfortunately, scrutiny of the disciplinary article has not taken place much beyond clergy couple circles. This is because the ruling has discriminated against clergy couples more than anyone else. A clergy couple at separate churches with separate parsonages may opt to live in one parsonage and lease out the other. In such a case the rent from the leased parsonage could be passed on to the pastor as a housing allowance. However, since neither housing nor a housing allowance is considered compensation, a local church is under no obligation to provide them if there is a house available to the pastor. Some local churches have taken advantage of this to deny income from a leased parsonage to clergy partners living in their spouse's parsonage.

These churches are following an interesting principle: when the opportunity exists to enable or deny extra income for the pastor, the church may deny it. This predisposition toward denial seems to say that pastors are not deserving of any advantage that the fortuitous availability of an extra parsonage may give them. There seems to be a belief that pastors' compensation is sufficient enough to justify excluding the opportunity for further income, which may be true of those pastors assigned to major congregations, but is hardly true for most clergy couple assignments. Clergy couples believe that both they and their ministries have been devalued by this ruling and the unfair practices it supports. If the purpose of a church's house is to "enable its ministry and the itinerant ministry of the Annual Conference," could not this enabling function be fulfilled through the translation of domicile space into supplementary income for the pastor? Clearly, the next General Conference faces one more justice issue in regard to clergy couples and the present ruling on housing.

We Can Celebrate

Clergy couples have had cause for celebration in the past. In 1973 the General Conference rescinded a clause that had since 1969 restricted pension credit to only the husband in a clergy couple. Now both partners are entitled to pension credit based on their respective service and also to death benefits provided by the deceased spouse's beneficiary clause. Furthermore, in 1988, entitlement to pension and death benefits was made retroactive for formerly excluded clergy couple partners.[4] Also, in 1988, the General Conference decreed that probationary members of the Annual Conference can qualify for elder's orders with less than full-time service; that change of status to less than full-time service can be requested with a lead time of only three months; and that two clergy can serve a single charge as co-pastors.

However, there is no disciplinary provision guaranteeing separate and equal health insurance coverage for each partner in a clergy couple, and though co-pastors are now a possibility, it is still required that one be designated "pastor-in-charge" for "administrative purposes."[5] These are matters that demand redressing. There have been sufficient changes for clergy couples to indicate that the church essentially has a heart of justice, and where injustice remains, we prefer to think that it is unintentional. But this is reason enough for clergy couples to make their voices heard.

A Little More Discipline, Please

The more pressing challenges for clergy couples are closer to home. Balancing the demands of church, spouse, and family, for instance, is a gauntlet hurled before us with daily frequency. It appears that the solution to the problem is personal discipline. We need discipline to protect and preserve our weekly days off, to say no to all encroachments on our annual vacation time, to intentionally schedule and keep time for leisure, recreation, and family interaction, to resist making one commitment after another, and to do all of these things without the usual guilt. Furthermore, we must be able at times to say "wait" to spouse and children and understand when our spouse says it to us. Striking any kind of balance is precarious, and this is no exception.

Resolving tensions within the partnership is another test of strength. The crucial element here is discernment. For clergy couples especially, tensions can have their source in either the merger of lives or the merger of ministries. The latter case is possible especially if there is significant differences between the styles and understanding of ministry. Tensions can be resolved by separating the two ministries if they are together or by even less involvement in the other's ministry if they are already separate. Here is an important benefit of equal claim upon the itineracy system. Clergy couples need to be able to discern whether tension lies in the marriage itself or in the conjoining of ministries.

Sometimes tension results when the otherwise proficient ministry of one partner is compromised by the inefficiency of the other. The options are to retain a conjoined ministry and strive for healing, or separate the ministries and allow each one to follow its course. Either decision can be a heartbreaking proposition. On the other hand, the healing of another's ministry is possible through involvement in it. Cabinets and Boards of Ordained Ministry have also begun to make counseling resources available to troubled clergy. The clergy couple must avoid getting trapped in a downward spiral. One spouse should not get pulled in by the other's undertow. The loving thing is to seek help, to find a way out, to find a way up.

Sometimes all efforts fail, even for clergy couple marriages. Undoubtedly, dissolution and divorce of a clergy couple entail reassignment of at least one but not necessarily both of the former partners. Allowing one of the divorced pastors to remain can actually lead to healing for that pastor and the congregation, but each situation should be allowed to dictate its own course of action. Fortunately, the days of automatic leaves of absence, loss of orders, and disgrace for divorced clergy are over. Automatic reassignment of divorced clergy is also passé. The climate of the church may, therefore, favor leaving one member of a former clergy couple in place if it is warranted by the best interests of the congregation and the conference.

If Whites Have a Cold, We Have the Flu

We have touched upon some critical matters. We are frustrated by not having enough space to deal with them more thoroughly. One final issue rises out of our experience as African-Americans. We hope that these discussions will have cross-cultural relevance, also. We must speak to the peculiar challenge of clergy couples who belong to global ethnic communities (a term we prefer to "ethnic minority groups"). There are relatively few African-American clergy couples. We are one of three African-American clergy couples in our conference as compared to seventeen Anglo-American clergy couples. We know of two interracial couples, one Asian couple, no Hispanic couples, and no Pacific-Islander couples in our conference. The situation may be analogous across the denomination.

The challenge of ethnic people who live in America may be best expressed by an old African-American adage, "If whites have a cold, we have the flu." In other words, the problems spilling over into our communities tend to be amplified and intensified by our legacy of discrimination and disadvantage. For us this is illustrated by the virtual nonexistence of congregations with an ethnic identity in our conference that are able to sustain a husband and wife clergy team. A failed experiment at assimilation has left many of our churches in a weakened and decimated condition. Many of our parsonages are aged, substandard dwellings in depressed neighborhoods. Many of our parishioners bear the psychic scars of victimization, and they show it when they come to church.

Those who are candidates for ordination continue to be frustrated by pressure to conform to a mostly white, male, and relatively affluent model of ministry. Many of our people are unaccustomed to women clergy. Strong patriarchal traditions hardened by a survival mentality make placement of women clergy difficult. Our memberships, as burdened as they are, feel imposed upon by the conference and its fiscal demands.

Furthermore, given the instability and fragility of many of our congregational situations, the itineracy has not been good for many of our churches. Frequent changes of pastors even in situations that were progressing well have demonstrated insensitivity to the need of our people for a stable pastoral relationship. We have been frustrated by hierarchical insensitivity to the peculiar shape that ministry must take in global ethnic communities. For example, pastors of global ethnic churches are usually invested with a higher degree of authority than pastors in Anglo-American congregations. The need and demand for authoritative leadership occurs naturally in survival situations, and global ethnic churches that are flourishing are characterized by authoritative pastoral leadership. Yet when global ethnic pastors must use their authority to solve problems caused by "broken" personalities within the church, they are often judged to be autocrats by culturally myopic members of the hierarchy looking in from the outside.[6] These pastors are subsequently transferred away from the church, usually against the wishes of the congregation's non-vocal majority who affirm and appreciate an authoritative leader.

On the other hand, some global ethnic pastors who need to be moved for the good of the church are left in place because they have learned not to make waves and are thus considered "good" ethnics. The fact that their congregations are languishing does not seem to matter much. Most pastors with an ethnic identity, however, are anguished over the state of their churches, and in their efforts to respond to the needs of their people they find themselves at odds with a system that imposes a culturally foreign model of ministry. When both husband and wife are at odds with the system, as is often the case with clergy couples, and particularly with those who belong to ethnic groups, then marital stress is also compounded.

What are we asking for by raising these issues? We ask only for understanding. Our clergy colleagues, particularly those having superintendency over us, should understand that most global ethnic churches are crisis situations where "business as usual" is no longer appropriate. Pastoral leadership must often take a shape that is radically different from that of Anglo-American ministry because the needs and problems are radically different. An understanding of this context would allow healing ministries time enough to develop in global ethnic situations. The development of such ministries would no longer be prematurely curtailed by fiat of the cabinet at the first sign of crisis in the congregation. Clergy and clergy couples of global ethnic communities usually possess the faith and spiritual resources to deal with the crises of their churches, neighborhoods, and families.

We Are Asking for Sensitivity, Not Expertise

Clergy couples from global ethnic communities have some challenges that are distinct from those of clergy couples in

Anglo-American communities. Still, in terms of importance, it is not our intention to exaggerate the challenges of the former nor minimize those of the latter. Our intention is only to expand our vision of the entire clergy couple phenomenon and the challenges facing us. Indeed, an expanded vision will still disclose experiences that challenge clergy couples across cultural lines. However, we must never lose sight of the experiential diversity that characterizes clergy couples in The United Methodist Church. Within this diversity lies the promise and potentiality of vital leadership for a multifaceted church.

While it is true that the presence of clergy couples offers little respite to an itineracy system that would rather not be disturbed, there is still meager justification for the view that clergy couples are a problem. It is not the problematic aspect of our presence, but the potentiality of our presence for positive ministry that confronts the itineracy system and coaxes it to change. Specifically, we are urging that the itineracy network first adopt a more positive attitude toward clergy couple appointments; second, distribute financial and housing resources in a way that is more supportive of clergy couples; and finally, become more sensitive to clergy couple experiences across the cultural board. We are asking only for sensitivity, not expertise, and it would help if bishops and cabinets listened more. If the itineracy system yields to change, an occurrence that appears inevitable, then the whole of the church will benefit from a more effective deployment of our ordained personnel, particularly by the appointments of clergy couples.

CHAPTER 11

Liberation for a Culture in Crisis

Rebecca S. Chopp

"I'm sorry. I do understand, but I am sorry. The church needs ministers like you." Those were the only words I could think to say when Sue called me to tell me she planned to leave the ministry at the end of the conference year. My heart was grieved, not only for Sue and the church, but also because Sue was one more of the many colleagues I have had in the United Methodist ministry who decided to leave.

As a teacher of United Methodist seminarians, I often look at my classes and know that some of the most talented will stay only briefly in the ministry. I know that most singles, the majority of women, many African-Americans and Hispanics, and some of the European-American married men will find the form and shape of ministry "in the real world" impossible to sustain with their bodies and souls. Almost all will be told that theology (that is, what they learned in seminary) does not matter compared to managing the church. Almost all will be forced to neglect their own spirituality in order to tend to the cares and needs of members of the church.

In our conversation, Sue told me about her struggle to decide to leave. She narrated the story of her burning concerns for mission, of her deep commitment to the church as a community of disciples, and of her intentions to develop rich, sustaining, and challenging worship experiences. Then she talked of her frustrations in trying to carry out this calling. Laity wanted her to meet their needs; denominational executives cared more about filling out forms than helping out in mission; and her seminary education equipped her with high ideals rather than with transforming practices. When she discussed her decision with other clergy, they responded by calling into question her commitment and loyalty to "the Methodist system." So Sue left, unsure of how to make sense of the difference between what she believed about ministry and the church and how she experienced ministry and the church in "the Methodist system."

Sue has been on my mind as I worked on this chapter, in which I was asked to address the topic "learning from voices of dissent." I was encouraged to give voice to those who have been hurt and excluded in the system of itineracy, as well as to describe alternative perspectives found in feminist and liberation theologies.[1] But with every attempt to center upon the notion of "dissent," my words appeared on the paper as a voice of challenge and hope. From a feminist and liberationist perspective, the questions posed in this book concern not only polity questions, or only life-style questions (as important as those questions are), but how we understand the mission and ministry of the church in our day.

According to feminists and liberationists, the basic problem with the church and ministry today is that sin is not denounced and grace is not announced. More specifically, feminist and liberation theologies contend that the cultural, social, and personal forms of destruction are not critically analyzed in the church. In addition, new systems, relations, and visions of human flourishing are not coming from the church. Thus what is most important from a feminist and liberationist perspective in a discussion of itineracy is to review the present mission and ministry of the church. In order to do this, I need to demystify the perception of the itineracy as some ahistorical "essential" form of ministry and examine it as a set of historical practices that at various times has served the mission of the church. My contention is that itineracy has one basic requirement: ministry must be shaped in order to adequately serve the mission of the church in the contemporary period. When I have established the basic principle of itineracy, I will need to examine the modern church and ministry, that is, the context in which most United Methodist churches exist and most ministers serve.

The issue facing The United Methodist Church is not simply updating the way it appoints its ministers, but how to change the modern form of ministry in which ministers are forced to be primarily caretakers and managers, and in which the church exists as a cult of subjectivity and a cult of bureaucracy. Then I will consider the challenges feminist and liberation theology present to our modern context, including how these theologies become voices of hope for the church and ministry.

The Historical Practices of Itineracy

E. Dale Dunlap, in an unpublished paper entitled "The System of Itineracy in American Methodism," suggests that itineracy has a pragmatic justification in The United Methodist Church.[2] There is nothing theological or religious or scriptural within the system of itineracy, contends Dunlap, for it started as a historical practice that fit the needs of the church as Methodism sought to live out its missionary impulse in serving churches across the land. Indeed, the fact that it has no special theological or scriptural justification is quite "Wesleyan," since Wesley was prone to call attention to the principles that the organizations had to serve. In other words, for Wesley the organization received its justification by serving the ends of the religious requirements. Wesley stated his pragmatic justification in the negative as he dealt with Methodism's relation to the Church of England:

> That we have in a course of years, out of necessity, not choice, slowly and warily varied in some points of discipline, by preaching in the fields, by extemporary prayer, by employing lay preachers, by forming and regulating societies, and by holding yearly Conferences. But we did none of these things till we were convinced we could no longer omit them but at the peril of our souls.[3]

It is an interesting form of justification: form the organizations of church and ministry if the omission of them puts souls in peril. Stated more positively, the justification is pragmatic, that is, the warrants are the practical effects of a structure of ministry that allows Methodism to carry out its missionary impulse.

As was often the case with historical practices, confusion arose between loyalty to the means rather than the ends. John Wesley was prone to confuse the itineracy with obedience to himself and thus presented a tension that plagued the various forms of itineracy. Though itineracy was created to serve the ministry for the mission of the church, it often seemed that ministry and the mission of the church were created to serve the itineracy. Francis Asbury became tempted frequently to identify the itineracy, that is the particular form of itineracy in his day and age, as the mission of the church: "If the itinerant ministry had its beginning under the leadership of Wesley, it had its greatest development under the direction of Francis Asbury."[4]

From the beginning the itineracy was a system with enormous costs: broken health, impossibility of maintaining family life, financial hardships. Such costs, combined with changing social patterns in North America, required new structures of ministry that were labeled itineracy. Indeed, from a historical viewpoint, the itineracy is not one unified historical practice, but different historical practices that adapted the basic concern of mission and ministry to changing historical periods. At first, itinerants moved in circuits constantly, changing every three months, and rarely staying more than six months. After the passing of the frontier, the itineracy changed dramatically. With the introduction of localization the pastor settled in a charge, which became the norm. What Asbury had called the evil of locality became intrinsic to the definition of itineracy.

We observe, first, that itineracy was an ecclesial-social invention, intended to serve the ministry and mission of the church. Second, itineracy has, like other social systems, confused means and ends, thus elevating a particular form of itineracy with the ministry and mission of the church. Third, itineracy is not a long, unbroken cord; it has changed dramatically, being redefined through the localization of pastors, a practice that was once opposed.

The importance of itineracy is the flexibility it offers each historical period to best serve the mission of the church. What is dangerous about itineracy is the temptation to elevate one historical form of serving the mission of the church as "eternal."

The Church and Ministry Today

Some years ago I attended a "united" church, the blend of a United Methodist congregation, a Presbyterian congregation, and a United Church of Christ congregation. All three churches kept their polity intact, with the minister holding full membership in his or her denomination, and associate memberships in the other two denominations. In my first few months at the church I was filled with amazement. How could Presbyterians, United Methodists, and United Church of Christ worshipers go to church together Sunday after Sunday? Once in a while I thought I could see a little tug and pull. Presbyterians did tend to care a bit more about the proper order of service, while United Methodists leaned toward planning a lot of celebrations and special events. The United Church of Christ members often led the mission concerns for the local neighborhood. However, such emphases were minimal; by and large the three churches merged together, got along well, and were fairly indistinguishable in terms of their piety, worship, outreach, and fellowship. The polities were distinct, and some polities required more time on the part of the ministers, the secretaries, and a few of the very active laity than others, but the life of the church went on like any regular or denominational church.

I attended this church for eight years. Now whenever I begin to make broad claims about the uniqueness of United Methodist congregations, the image of the united church hovers in my consciousness. The united church is my personal example of a trend known quite well to sociologists, church leaders, and laity: mainline churches are often more alike than they are different. The nature of the church in the present age has to be understood not just in terms of its denominational affiliation and its own local history, but also through an analysis of the broader reality of church and ministry in America.

The context is the church in modernity, especially in the last thirty years. This context is spoken of by many authors and from many perspectives, from Robert Bellah to Martin Marty, from United Methodist bishops to Stanley Hauerwas. Liberation theologians, in the context of voices of challenge/voices of hope, often have a great deal to say about the church, both in terms of criticism and also of possibility. To avoid dismissing the analysis of context because it comes from a voice of dissent, I will portray the context from a voice that appeals to liberals, liberationists, and evangelicals in our churches: Jürgen Moltmann.

In *Theology of Hope,* Moltmann suggested that the modern church has been assigned three tasks: the cult of subjectivity, the cult of co-humanity, and the cult of the institution.[5] Moltmann explains that society has assigned, or allowed, the church to perform three basic functions. First, it caters to individual needs and wants; second, it serves as a place where lonely persons can go for fellowship, usually with like-minded persons; and third, it follows the bureaucratic structure of rationality for institutional governance.

Moltmann contended that the most important role assigned to religion, more specifically to Christianity, is the preservation of the individual, especially the maintenance of deep personal meanings.

and feelings of existential wholeness and well-being. Moltmann is especially correct here insofar as he is speaking about the mainline traditions, which have assumed that the locus of religion is in the individual and that religious experience has to do with connecting the individual, in some deeply mysterious manner, to God as the ultimate, the holy, the one beyond all limits. If theology has affirmed this in many different ways, the laity equally assume this. They come to church not to hear about politics or economics, but to have their own religious experience nurtured.

The second need Moltmann mentioned relates to this quite closely. Persons come to church to meet like-minded individuals in order to find some sense of community. Moltmann referred to this as a Noah's Ark syndrome, for it belies the deep, frightening loneliness of modernity. Increasingly, as our society becomes more transient, more people come to our church to form meaningful human contact. Yet I think it fair to subsume this second function of the church, the cult of co-humanity, into the first, the cult of subjectivity, for it has been filled by what the authors of *Habits of the Heart* called "lifestyle enclaves."[6] To be in community is, in most American churches, to be with persons who generally agree with you and who generally look like you (shared race and class).

homogeneous community

According to Moltmann, the third need, or function, that modernity assigned the church is to be a cult of institutionality. The organization is structured in itself and in relation to other organizations through modern practices of bureaucracy. In this way the church is part and parcel of modernity, with paid workers and trained staff organized to operate around principles of management and operational procedures. What were once denominational heritages, marked by theological richness, are now denominational organizations, marked by particular rationalistic practices. As a bureaucratic institution, the church organizes itself to do what bureaucratic organizations do—survive, tend the status quo, follow established procedures, and interrelate with other bureaucratic organizations.

Using Moltmann's analysis, it is also easy to sketch the contours of modern ministry. Contours is not meant as an exact representation of how every minister functions but rather the general historical forces influencing religion and other institutions that emphasize or make explicit certain dimensions of ministry. These forces include everything from the expectations of laity to how evaluation surveys get formed, from questions asked by Boards of Ministry to popular topics in literature on ministry. The first need requires modern ministry to focus on individual needs—that is, to meet the pastoral and spiritual needs of individuals in the church. The rising importance of pastoral care, which for many years was based on an individualistic, existential model, suggests how ministry has been formed in the modern period. Likewise, the theology of Barth, Tillich, Rahner, and Bultmann taught in seminaries in this country has been interpreted existentially. In this function the minister becomes a caregiver, in assuring the parishioners of their acceptance and worth and in treating their needs.

The third role of religion in the modern period, the cult of institution, has obviously formed ministry. Denominational organizations with their reports, ordination requirements, continuing education services, and management seminars force the habits of ministry into bureaucratic rationality. Like so many students, I was not quite prepared to leave seminary with its exciting array of social action, rich worship, and challenging theologies, to move into the bureaucracy, thus becoming a "company man," attending endless meetings, producing quarterly reports, and managing finances. I am not saying that this is bad or good, nor am I suggesting that it is the fault of any one person or group of persons. But it is a historical formation of ministry in the modern period. Ministers are both caretakers of individuals and managers of organizations.

We might ask ourselves at this point how the particularities of the itineracy system served the functions of the modern church. We will have to answer that it served it quite well. When itineracy moved to the practice of localized pastors, the connectional system served the bureaucracy well. With connecting links already in place, the itineracy could become a part of bureaucratic organization with great efficiency. And indeed, my travels into other denominations have taught me one thing about United Methodism—no one can organize as fully and completely as connectional systems!

The localization of clergy also fits into the modern task of focusing on individual needs, especially as the appointment process moved to a consulting system where bishops and their cabinets try to "fit" the gifts of ministers with the needs of churches. If a pastor-parish committee was unhappy with the minister, it was easy to move him or her to another parish. Likewise, if the parish did not fit the taste of a minister, one could adapt by asking for a lateral move. It must be said, and often is, that the connectional system of appointments gives ministers more freedom; they can speak their minds and not worry about being fired. In principle this is true, and I admire district superintendents and bishops for supporting ministers in their right to prophetically lead congregations. Unfortunately, most ministers move not because they are too prophetic, but because they do not visit enough, are not spiritual enough, or are just not the right type for that parish. Against these kinds of complaints, district superintendents and bishops find themselves in a very difficult position since the church in modernity is meant to serve individual needs and since the efficient bureaucracy of the United Methodist system makes it relatively easy to move ministers.

It has been said that the connectional system works better for those not represented in large numbers in ministry. At least for women, there is truth to this adage at entry level positions. It must also be said that there is no evidence that itineracy is helpful to women in middle or top level appointments. Indeed, I have wondered about the benefits to the women I know, who were helped through by sending them to small, struggling churches opposed to receiving a woman. At best, itineracy has been a "mixed bag" for women.

New Voices

Increasingly, feminist, black, and other liberation theologians are asking the church to rethink the nature and purpose of the church and ministry. Though I want to concentrate on their challenges to us, I also want to observe that the voices of liberationists speak in the midst of a crisis in mainline churches and a growing doubt, and even despair, among mainline clergy. I speak frequently to clergy groups, and address how liberation theology can be a resource. I am amazed at the hunger ministers feel for a sense of mission and calling, for a stirring of spiritual power and social action, for a challenge to give their vocation and profession new life in the midst of a troubled culture. Ministers are weary of the caretaking and management functions they have been assigned in the modern church. While not denying the importance of the church as an institution of service, ministers today wonder whether this is all there is to the gospel. Are we speaking to the real cultural problems or simply sticking on bandages? How is the church different from social service agencies? In what way is Christ in our midst calling us to go into the world?

Feminist and liberation theologies present two fundamental assumptions: first, our culture is in crisis, by which I mean the physical crisis of the poor and oppressed, the psychic crisis of American individualism, and the environmental crisis of our physical life; and second, the church must undergo emancipation and transformation in order to speak to the crises of American culture and to provide new visions for human flourishing. I will examine both of these assumptions in turn.

First, as we observe the crises of global conflict, economic recession, and rising rates of addictive behavior on our streets and in our homes, we sense that something is wrong. Leftist prophets and persons on the fringes of our society are not alone in saying that the social system is deeply troubled. Indeed, critics from right and left agree that we need dramatic change.

We are experiencing major problems with our social systems and structures, such as health care, education, politics, and welfare, and the structures of family and of marriage are in deep crisis. It is now common parlance to speak of our culture as an addictive society. Such language tempts trivialization of the fact that millions of persons suffer such deep psychic pain that they can find no relief other than drugs, alcohol, sex, or shopping. This indicates, I think, that the structures of subjectivity—the visions and forms of being human—are also in crisis.

Seeing the present cultural crisis as the context for a discussion of the itineracy may seem odd, but ministry and itineracy are deeply tied to the present historical context in their nature and purpose. How do we in the ministry of the church address the crisis which is the concern of our present mission, and form a system of ministry that fills this mission?

In order to address the cultural crises and to denounce sin and announce grace, the modern church and its ministry need to be extricated from the forms and expectations of ministry and to conceive new visions.

Second, the church must experience emancipation and transformation to serve its mission in the present day. One example of this mission is the treatment of addictive disorders. I am amazed at the inability of modern ministry to analyze and address the massive addiction in our society. As I travel across the country, I rarely find in-depth spiritual analysis of addiction in the churches. Indeed, if one wants to hear addiction treated as a spiritual problem, one must trundle down to the church basement where a local chapter of Alcoholics Anonymous often meets on Sunday evening. Yet the Christian community upstairs represents an incredible tradition of spiritual power, the ordering of desires, and compulsive behavior. As an alternative, Augustine provided rich resources to speak of addiction. Augustine was deeply concerned about the order of desires in the soul and contended that when the heart is not in God, then the desires of the soul fall into disarray, and destructive behavior to others and to the self occurs. The soul racked in pain seeks to soothe its agony and achieve some symptomatic relief.[7]

The churches fail to call on such rich analyses of addiction and thus contribute to the work of Twelve-Step programs. We also fail to call on the transforming grace of the proper ordering of desires, as Augustine discovered. We remain caught in the culture of individual subjectivity, where the point of religion is not to order the soul's desires, but to affirm its acceptance by God. There is an important difference between telling individuals week after week a religious version of "you're ok, I'm ok, we're all ok," and offering them a strong spiritual analysis of the desires of the heart. Americans have become diseased by focusing on "soothers" instead of facing their pain. I am not saying that God does not accept us; indeed, part of God's acceptance, from an Augustinian perspective, is that in God we have the strength to face our pain, to go through the abyss of our denial and despair, and to find new visions for wholeness.

Churches must become communities of deliverance for themselves. Like some of the African-American churches in our urban areas, they must utilize the resources of Christian tradition and equip themselves with the spiritual and theological tools to diagnose the sins and to anoint God's grace, which, Johannes Baptist Metz has suggested, "is a way of living differently."[8]

I will comment on feminist theology, with the reminder that African American, Latin American, and other forms of liberation theology also have a great deal to offer. Feminist theology, at least for the purpose of this chapter, suggests that the church and ministry must question the systems and structures of destruction. Feminist theology analyzes how present patriarchal culture has rigidly defined rules and roles for persons and how it has helped contribute to massively unjust social systems. But in the midst of this denunciation, feminist theology provides us with a view of being human that is defined through mutuality, embodiment, and relation to the earth. It offers, also, a process of living in community that stresses naming one's world, living justly in relationships, and proclaiming the possibilities of living anew in the midst of God's world. It gives us new ways of understanding and of acting: understanding that order requires a balance with creativity, enacting power as the ability to have one's part matter, and relating to the earth as friend rather than as master.

Itineracy

What does all this have to do with itineracy? The itineracy is a set of historical practices that, at various times in our history, have been shaped to serve the mission of the church. Thus, in order to discuss the itineracy, it is necessary to discuss the mission of the church. Within this context we can begin to understand the nature and shape of ministry.

If the church needs to form communities of emancipation and transformation, then ministry in the future needs to focus on how it enables and leads these communities. We need a structure of ministry that enables ministers to be moral leaders in analyzing and transforming local situations. In order to fulfill our mission, we must have a structure of ministry in which ministers will not just maintain institutions, but will become community formers by using the traditions and practices of Christianity to help persons form new communities in which they can live justly and experience renewal.

We must explore together how we shape our ministry for the present age. My plea is that we stick with the question long enough to explore it well, and that we refuse the easy route of uncoupling the discussion of the structure of itineracy from the discussion of the nature of our mission. The voices of challenge confront us with allowing the questions regarding itineracy to address the questions regarding our mission. The voices of hope confront us with the fact that this is both possible and necessary in the present day.

Where Do We Go from Here?

Donald E. Messer

At the height of the civil rights struggle, when Martin Luther King, Jr., entitled a book *Where Do We Go From Here,* he appended a subtitle offering the option of *Chaos or Community?* The crisis of confidence in the United Methodist itineracy system probably does not warrant an apocalyptic choice between chaos or covenant, but it does urge the denomination to address the pressing theological and practical questions threatening to paralyze the church's mission and ministry. King's prophetic words, however, seem to be appropriate: "We are now faced with the fact that tomorrow is today. We are confronted with the fierce urgency of *now.* In this unfolding conundrum of life and history there is such a thing as being too late. Procrastination is still the thief of time. Life often leaves us standing bare, naked and dejected with a lost opportunity."[1]

The preceding chapters, written by fourteen lay and clergy authors representative of a broad spectrum of church opinion, underscore this crisis of confidence and urge for reform, if not revolution, in the way itineracy functions in the future. Basically, the redemptive renewal, not the radical removal, of itineracy is advocated. The debate neither began nor will it end with this volume, but in the hopeful words of Bishop Roy I. Sano, the book "will loosen up the soil for planting seeds of new options."[2] In that spirit, this chapter will explore the possibilities of re-visioning the itinerant image of ministry, revising itineracy's assumptions, and revitalizing itineracy for a renewed church. Where we go from here literally depends upon the *laos,* the whole people of God called United Methodists.

Re-visioning the Itinerant Image of Ministry

Images shape human behavior at deep, often subliminal levels. Mental portraits of ministry possess an evocative power that can touch attitudes and transform action. Images of ministry can inflame our imaginations and provide identities. Images, however, can be based on misunderstandings and misreadings of history and, in essence, be "dead metaphors" inappropriate for the contemporary church and world.[3] Illustrative is the stereotypical itinerant image of ministry associated with the early circuit rider.

Nineteenth-century Methodist biographers and historians assiduously cultivated and enriched the romantic image of the circuit rider as hero.[4] The incomparable sacrifices and services of these historic figures are neither to be denied nor denigrated by an overcritical realism. The results of their evangelistic efforts were amazing. Only eighty-three circuit riders and 15,000 lay ministers labored in 1784. By 1840 one of every nineteen United States citizens was a Methodist.[5] Other denominations registered frequent complaints, however, against these zealous Methodist preachers because of their ecumenical insensitivities, especially when their evangelism became proselytization based on false portrayals of other's cherished beliefs and practices.[6]

As writers in this book have documented repeatedly, itineracy in its infancy was an inhumane system, destructive of many human lives and values. Episcopal authoritarianism, often projected as God's will, prevailed. Truly it represented "a system of sacrifice." Young male circuit riders may have offered themselves "without reserve," but they frequently suffered inordinate illnesses and early death. In 1847 almost half died before they reached thirty-five years of age and two-thirds before they had completed twelve years of service.[7] Those who were married often neglected wives and families due to excessive travel and lack of material resources (epitomized by the destitute clergy widow).

The image of itinerant ministry has always been associated with travel, with moving from place to place, and with breaking beyond borders. In re-visioning contemporary ministry as cross-cultural, it is imperative to recall that traversing racial, gender, and cultural boundaries has not always been a high objective of itineracy. Racism and sexism, for example, were accepted realities. The church excluded women not only from being circuit riders, but until relatively recently from the ordained ministry and many other significant roles in the church.

In 1784 the Christmas Conference took a prophetic stance against slavery, but by 1785 it backtracked, because in Thomas Coke's words, "We thought it prudent to suspect the minute concerning slavery, on account of the great opposition that had been given it, our work being in too infantile a state to push things to extremity." Prudence triumphed over the prophetic in the name of evangelism and church growth.[8]

Itineracy proved disastrous in evangelizing and ministering to Native Americans. Frequent changes of appointments and insensitivity to cultural differences, spiritual values, and language differences made itinerant pastors generally irrelevant and ineffective.[9] A re-visioned image of itinerant ministry needs to understand traveling as more than moving from parish to parish, but also crossing cultural barriers of race, gender, and class.

Demythologizing the circuit riders becomes necessary, lest the church view today's clergy as morally worse than previous generations. Modern itinerants demonstrate in every way their value as worthy successors of yesterday's circuit riders. Circuit riders also were fragile and fallible human beings. They were not giants but persons of uneven stature, with passions and temptations similar to our own. Loneliness prevailed and alcoholism was not infrequent, with martyrs to peach brandy not unknown.[10] One suspects other typical human peccadillos; immunity from the sins of the flesh and spirit seem unlikely. Church trials of clergy rebelling from dictatorial discipline happened frequently, and the excessive clergy "turnover" employment rates hardly represent models of efficiency and effectiveness, much less humaneness and harmony. From the beginning of American Methodism to 1814, about 63 percent of the 1,616 traveling preachers no longer served as circuit riders due to location, death, resignation, or expulsion.[11]

Today the heroic circuit rider image illustrates a dead metaphor, hopelessly distorted and haplessly dated. Romanticizing the itinerant image of the circuit rider can have dysfunctional influence on the contemporary church and clergy. Making the legends of early preachers larger than life engenders unnecessary guilt. Extolling their personal and sacrificial virtues for the sake of upbuilding the church often overlooks their failure, and that of the system, to care appropriately for their spouses and children. Impoverished families are a type of spouse and child abuse that should not be glorified by the church. The lingering legacy of the heroic circuit rider sometimes spotlights inappropriate images both of itineracy and mission, no longer appropriate for the twenty-first century.

In re-imaging itinerant ministry, the vital roles and responsibilities of laity also need highlighting. Histories of itineracy have suffered from clerical myopia, often overlooking the essential ministry of the laity which made early itineracy effective. In fact, the majority of the circuit riders themselves were laity. Not until 1784 was there a single ordained minister in all of American Methodism. Active lay women and men led the communities of faith they established and visited. They were the local preachers, exhorters, and class leaders.[12] How presumptuous it is to credit itinerant clergy with the remarkable early church growth without equal emphasis on the ministry of the laity.

The future vitality of United Methodism depends upon laity, who are theologically astute, spiritually committed, and who understand the vocation of the priesthood of all believers. Laity as partners with the clergy in ministry will create a more dynamic connectional itineracy.

In reconstructing a new itinerant image of ministry, The United Methodist Church needs to remember and to appropriate its entire heritage, not just its dominant Methodist tradition. The United Brethren Church had a different itinerant system than the Methodists. Preachers could still have full conference rights even if they chose not to travel. In contrast to the average four-year tenure of today's United Methodist clergy, United Brethren leader Philip Otterbein stayed at the same station for forty years!

Likewise, from the very beginning, the Evangelical Association had city preachers who did not itinerate and who earned larger salaries than those who traveled. Raymond Albright spoke of the difference in itinerant systems as the stumbling stone to union of the two denominations in the early 1800s.[13] When re-visioning our image of itinerant ministry for contemporary times, it is imperative to recall the totality of our history.

After all, the initial pattern of itineracy is not the ethical or ecclesiastical norm for all time. Stanley J. Menking says the contemporary church is experiencing the maturation and evolution of itineracy, not its demise. Just as itineracy adapted to new demands and situations in the past, it will adjust to overcome current stresses and strains, such as those challenges offered by contributors to this book.[14] Rebecca S. Chopp notes that "the itineracy is not one unified historical practice, but different historical practices that accepted the basic concern of mission and ministry to changing historical periods. Itineracy in the past has changed to meet the mission of the church, just as it must now change to serve a new mission."

A genuine itinerant system ended with the abolition of time limits late in the nineteenth century. As early as 1840 seventy "travelling" preachers actually served in special appointments, teaching in the colleges. By 1880 three hundred clergy were in "virtual location" due to special appointments. What are now somewhat pejoratively called "appointments beyond the local church" (tending to give a second-class status to vital clergy appointments) were recognized as integral to itineracy even though not subject to the same time limits and appointment processes. This exception to itineracy has not always pleased episcopal authorities, but since the system's primary purpose has been meeting human needs, remarkable flexibility has evolved.

The itinerant ministry changes as needs change. As Russell E. Richey has demonstrated, it is an absolute myth "that the ministry in the old days, the ministry we knew in our youth, the ministry that we have heard about—was esteemed, was effective, possessed authority, transformed people and congregations, was undaunted by the challenges it faced, preached with vigor and conviction, was untempted by worldly, family, financial considerations."[15]

The "old song" of pastoral declension or deterioration has been sung about preachers ever since the second generation of New England pastors emerged. Change, not decline, best describes styles of ministry and clergy over the centuries. And change will characterize the future as we re-vision the itinerant image of ministry.

Revising Itineracy's Assumptions

Six assumptions compose the bedrock of United Methodism's system of itineracy. These primary presuppositions have been basic to the debate articulated by the contributors to this book and are critical in future deliberations. Some re-visioning of these assumptions has already evolved. A key issue is how much more re-visioning must yet occur.

The first assumption underscores the connectional vs. congregational nature of the denomination since congregations do not have the right to choose their own clergy. Clergy maintain membership in the Annual Conference, not a local congregation. No local church stands alone, but each is spiritually bonded and legally bound one to another. Final decisions regarding the selection, ordination, and appointment of clergy abide not with a single congregation but with the denominational connection which includes all congregations.

An anomaly of the connectional itinerant system has long been the tendency of larger congregations to "call" their pastors, with the "consent" of the bishop. As early as 1842 Elijah Hedding lamented that unless this increasing practice abated—"both of the preachers and people, for certain places and certain men"—itineracy could not long survive.[16] Yet the church to this day continues to struggle with the tensions of this dilemma. The basic itinerant system has prevailed despite the undermining impact of what the bishops condemned in 1912 as "congregational episcopacy."[17]

A new image and understanding of Christian ministry must combine the indispensable partnership of both laity and clergy. The *laos,* the people of God, do not welcome passive roles in determining who will serve as their pastors. Some affirm with George Bernard Shaw that all professions are "conspiracies against the laity."[18] Laity will assume a larger role and responsibility in matters of United Methodist itineracy.

Whether this means a voice and a choice for laity in selecting United Methodist pastors for their churches is yet to be determined, but increased involvement in the system of itineracy seems inevitable and desirable. Research in Florida and elsewhere indicates laity do not necessarily want a call system, but they do want to participate.[19] Other congregations now demand what historically has been a prerogative of high-steeple churches. A new generation of laity in small membership churches increasingly refuse to trust or to accept a guaranteed appointment system that imposes upon them pastors whose "gifts, graces, faith and fruits" appear "light miles" from what their congregations and communities need and deserve.

Salaries have already moved from a connectional to a congregational-oriented basis with consequent missional implications. Salary considerations rather than missional motivations appear to dominate appointment making in many conferences. Donald H. Treese lists it as only one important factor in the process, but studies such as the one in the Florida Annual Conference reveal that laity and clergy both believe it is "the most important factor in making appointments."[20] This finding can be replicated almost universally.

Initially, a structure of equal compensation, designed to meet bare necessities with no thought for tomorrow, formed the basis of itinerant salaries. Francis Asbury received the same as his traveling preachers. In 1792 circuit rider salaries were fixed at $64 plus traveling expenses. Wives also received $64 "if they be in want of it." "A brotherhood of poverty" prevailed.[21] In making appointments, differential salaries from place to place were not a factor, thus enabling Methodists to serve impoverished people or establish new mission outposts.

Gradually, changes in equal compensation for salaries and expenses developed. By 1860 the General Conference of the Methodist Episcopal Church had decreed each Quarterly Conference could determine the preacher's salary. In the latter half of the nineteenth century, all the predecessary denominations moved away from connectionalism toward a more congregational-oriented system of paying pastors. By 1915, the system in place today had already evolved.

Bishops in the United States all receive the same salaries. District superintendents within a conference have similar salaries with modest differentials. Missionaries and staff in national and conference offices are paid within established salary ranges. Connectional commands govern the minimal compensation for pastor, but congregational considerations determine upper limits. Lyle E. Schaller blames minimal salaries for reducing the missional outreach of larger membership congregations, while Donald H. Treese champions basic salaries as a means for missional renewal.

Schaller asks whether itineracy now serves primarily the clergy rather than the church. Certain financial statistics could suggest that conclusion but closer analysis of financial data reveals a different perspective. In a recent year, United Methodists contributed to Annual Conference and general church funds $230 million for clergy support and $257 million for mission benevolences. In contrast, fifteen years ago the church gave almost 100 percent more for outreach than for clergy support. Pension and health insurance costs largely account for this dramatic increase, combined with only a 53 percent increase in mission contributions. During the same time period, pastors' salaries and expenses have almost tripled (from $215 to $623 million). Lest it appear that clergy have suddenly become wealthy, one should note that based on inflationary-adjusted dollars, the increase amounts to $234 million, up only 7 percent in fifteen years.[22]

What may have occurred, though some dispute the claim, is a

greater discrepancy between the salaries and benefits of the lowest-paid and highest-paid pastors both within and between conferences.[23] Especially alarming is the glaring gap between salaries and benefits of Anglo-American pastors and ethnic pastors, which continually widens. In addition, poorer congregations often hide inability to pay pension and/or health insurance costs, note Bonnie J. Messer and Denise Johnson Stovall, with spouses and children as victims of a flawed itineracy.[24]

A second historic assumption of itineracy is that the ordained clergy have no right to choose their own fields of labor. Just as congregations forsake their right to choose their own pastors, the clergy yield their prerogatives about where they will be deployed to serve.

Since 1972, consultation has been required with a pastor and a parish before the consummation of an appointment. Open to many definitions, this rule represents the most recent "liberalization" of the itineracy system. Actually it began in the 1940s when the *Discipline* first instructed district superintendents to consult with pastors, if possible, before making appointments. Some fear consultation may lead to a "call" system, and that the laity expect consultation to evolve into a system in which the pastor-parish committee will select the preacher. Or perhaps consultation may represent simply a half-way step to a call system, that will ultimately prevent laity from having either a voice or a choice in making appointments.

Dictionaries suggest *consultation* means to "ask the advice or opinion of" others or "to deliberate together" or "to have regard to the opinion or perspective of another." The *Discipline* of The United Methodist Church fails to clarify the process of consultation, raising the possibility for rampant misunderstanding and abuse. In one instance, the Judicial Council ruled that a bishop posting appointments on a bulletin board prior to reading them aloud was not considered consultation![25]

In general, clergy and their families, and the parishes they serve, are defenseless against varying interpretations of the meaning of consultation. It is not uncommon when bishops change for people to confront a totally new explanation of the meaning of itineracy. Saying no when asked to move may be graciously received by one episcopal leader, while another bishop resents such impudence, believing that such clergy break the covenant, undermine the system, and fail to offer themselves "without reserve."

When M. Kent Millard proposes a renewed emphasis on spiritual discernment of the will of God for a given church, the interesting question is how the pastor and the parish involved join with the bishop and cabinet in the divine consultation process. One pastor told me that he once declined a campus ministry appointment only to be summoned to the bishop's office. Seated behind his desk, the bishop declared, "When I and the twelve men on my cabinet make a decision, we believe it is due to the guidance of the Holy Spirit." Not overwhelmed, the young pastor replied that he did not think "their Holy Spirit had all the facts and that his Holy Spirit told him to remain an associate pastor." He stayed in that parish, later transferring to another conference where today he pastors one of the fastest growing new congregations in the United States.

A set of guidelines explicating and clarifying the meaning of consultation is urgently needed. A connectional system with seventy-two different conference interpretations of consultation, which fluctuate with the assignments of bishops, hardly respects the integrity of parishes or clergy and their families. Few question the need for ultimate authority to rest with the bishop, but almost everyone fears episcopal authoritarianism contrary to the spirit of covenant.

The person and role of the district superintendent are clearly critical in the consultative process. The size of many conferences precludes the possibility of a bishop's knowing intimately the hopes and needs of the pastor, the parish, and the congregation. How often district superintendents are gifted or trained in consultation remains unknown, but one suspects substantial room for improvement.

Bishop Nolan B. Harmon contends that the first two classic assumptions demand a *third*, namely: *"That the appointment be made by a competent, impartial, untrammeled authority (the bishop), whose powers and duties must be outlined carefully and ordered by the whole church."*[26] The contributors to this book questioned neither the competence nor the impartial integrity of the denomination's bishops. United Methodists generally have great respect for the episcopal office and deep appreciation for the women and men who currently have been elected to serve as bishops. They are more than worthy successors to those who preceded them.

However, the amount of authority and power accorded to the office has drastically changed since the inception of itineracy and the episcopacy. Holding the office of bishop requires making tough decisions, but, as I indicated in the book's introduction, contemporary bishops often feel more like Jonathan Swift's Gulliver, shackled by six-inch-tall Lilliputians, rather than persons possessing "untrammeled authority." Does itineracy require a powerful episcopacy? In previous eras, bishops operated with an authoritarian administrative style, but today's episcopal leaders are expected to be servant-leaders. Authority comes not automatically, but must be gained or earned by demonstrating a caring, competent leadership that incarnates the love of the gospel.

The mood of the denomination is not to eliminate the episcopacy or to devalue its authority to set appointments and to provide visionary leadership. Likewise, the prevailing spirit is not to restore arbitrary powers or to tolerate leaders who are not collegial and caring.

Clerical persons are not chess pieces to be moved capriciously at the whim and fancy of cabinets and congregations. At some points in history clergy and their families literally did not know where they were going until the very last minute when the presiding bishop read off the appointments at Annual Conference. The day of secrecy and last-minute pastoral announcements no longer exists.

The only remaining entrails of this system now occur ironically with the sudden and secret assignment of bishops to areas of service! Without explanation, episcopal families expecting to live in Chicago may find themselves appointed to Fargo! The windows to the closed deliberations of jurisdictional episcopal committees should be opened in order to allow for less time-pressured decision making and to encourage greater sensitivity to spouses. If clergy and laity want more considerate consultation and less arbitrary authoritarianism, they might begin by humanizing the way that bishops are assigned to areas of service. A theologically sound ministry at all levels must always be rooted in respect for human dignity and autonomy. As Rabbi Samuel E. Karff has written: "Ministry that is shaped by this theologically informed principle will be compassionate, sensitive, understanding, participatory, and representative of God's ministry."[27] What a great description of an ideal bishop!

The fourth basic condition of itineracy is the ideal of covenant. The Christian church is a covenantal community, and ours is a covenant ministry of grace. Regulatory rules and systems for disciplining ministry always exist in church organizations, but they are a fragile framework compared to a trusting, covenantal understanding of ministry rooted in relationship to Christ and the personal conscience of every person.

Many believe that this sense of covenant is nearly non-existent among itinerant clergy today. A renewed sense of covenant among pastors in the connection emerges as a high priority. William B. Oden, Donald H. Treese, and M. Kent Millard particularly stress the disciplinary note referring to the covenant that should bond clergy in the connection. Russell E. Richey suggests it was once historically present, though Bonnie J. Messer and Denise Johnson Stovall argue that past covenants were often based on an unequal and unfair balance in power.

Years ago, I noted that people do not pontificate or legislate for hypothetical situations. Signs are not erected for non-existent problems. When as president of Dakota Wesleyan University I visited the music school, I noted the professors posted announcements asking, "Please pick up your music," but in the athletic department the bulletin boards read, "Don't spit on the floor!" The clamor over covenant reveals a serious issue. The absence of a genuine feeling of covenant is problematic for United Methodism. What Prentiss M. Gordon, Sr., discovered doing research in contemporary Mississippi is echoed across the denomination:

> Covenant among United Methodist clergypersons is not thought or felt to be present to any significant degree. It is deeply desired and felt to be much needed. It would be a revolutionary thing for good if it could and were to happen. A lack of this tends to threaten our self-image and sense of integrity. . . . Appointments are too often perceived as being made on the basis of playing favorites and by playing politics on the part of bishops and district superintendents and clergypersons, with the bishops and district superintendents being perceived as feeling that they are superior persons to those "in the trenches."[28]

In conferences stratified by major differences in salaries between pastors, the covenant idea may be more difficult to maintain and nurture. British Methodists who still itinerate on circuits and serve with colleagues in a variety of congregations may find the experience of covenant more relevant to their situations.

Unmarried circuit riders could pledge themselves "without reserve," but today most pastors experience conflicting covenants. A Tennessee pastor and clergy couple partner, Mary Virginia Taylor, notes:

> It is impossible to take the covenant language about offering yourself without reserve literally. The reality is that we are in more than one

covenant. My marriage covenant was not simply made with my husband, but it was also made with God.[29]

Since the disciplinary language about covenanting to offer oneself "without reserve" is being killed "by a thousand qualifications" like marriage, children, personal independence, Thomas H. C. McArthur questions whether the language should not be deleted, fearing "what happens to an organization that continues to give lip service to words but doesn't really live by them."[30]

A fifth assumption of itineracy promises a pulpit for every preacher and a cleric for every congregation. The pride of connectional United Methodism has been the ability to fill all pastorates and to employ all pastors. This system maximizes the effective deployment of persons with diverse talents. When congregations relinquish their right to choose their own pastor, and pastors give up their right to choose their own congregation, effective matches of pulpit and preacher can be swiftly and appropriately finalized.

Horace G. Smith, however, suggests we have overworked the notion that every clergyperson is "entitled to an appointment and need to re-emphasize the corollary that every church is entitled to a competent pastor."[31] The moral and legal implications of imposing an ineffective or incompetent (or worse yet an immoral) pastor on an unsuspecting congregation have barely been explored.

In this book, Donald H. Treese expresses confidence that current church regulations provide an effective means of dealing with the pastor who no longer functions effectively. William B. Oden emphasizes the value and importance of reclaiming these persons for ministry. Speaking from a lay perspective, Sally B. Geis feels less certain that the church provides a way to protect local congregations from disastrous appointments, which wreak havoc with the lives of people and programs. Geis, however, questions abolishing guaranteed appointments. She fears that the prophetic, rather than the pathetic, pastors might be the first to lose their position.

Joon Kwan Un reports and Lyle E. Schaller proposes radical alternatives to eliminating guaranteed appointments. Such alternatives would not be easy to swallow if we note some shocking statistics from the Southern Baptist convention, a group that settles conflict in ways that create chaos for the clergy. A 1990 report found that in the past eighteen months, 2,100 pastors had been fired—a 31 percent increase over what occurred six years earlier. A Missouri study showed that most pastors did not even know they were going to be fired before it happened. Reportedly, "the most insecure person in the world is a Baptist minister in his 50s who's having trouble in his church."[32]

If itineracy and guaranteed appointments are to retain credibility and viability, this dilemma must be addressed effectively and quickly. Every conference has, or acknowledges having, pastors clearly unsuited for the parish ministry, but bishops are forced to move them routinely from place to place, waiting for the next congregation to be disrupted, if not destroyed. Sometimes the minimum salary funds subsidize failure.[33] The smaller and weaker the community of faith, the more likely they are to suffer from this game of episcopal roulette. Humane, but expeditious, systems of support and re-education must be developed immediately to enable pastors to exit with dignity and to resume their ministry apart from the clerical office.

Long courtships are preferable to short marriages. By guarding the gate where persons enter conference membership, the vast majority of future personnel problems can be reduced. Increased lay participation and empowerment in processes that prevent inappropriate and ill-prepared persons entrance into the clergy profession is anticipated. Instead of operating with a "closed-shop" mentality, clergy ought to welcome learned laity into decisions that determine future pastors and appointments. Resistance is inevitable. When students in colleges and seminaries first secured voting rights in faculty selection processes, people claimed the consequences would be catastrophic. Likewise, after the appointment of members to state boards regulating particular professions, observers expressed concern that the laity would lower standards. In truth, both innovations led to higher quality decision making and are seldom questioned. Greater involvement of and voting powers for all the *laos* in boards of ministry at all levels will enhance, not eviscerate, ministry and itineracy.

A sixth *premise of itineracy is that there is an equality of opportunity for every itinerant to serve in any place.* This constitutes the great promise of itineracy in a connectional church, a very attractive feature for bright and promising persons becoming clergy.

Unfortunately, few promises have been betrayed more often. Susan M. Morrison and Gilbert H. Caldwell personally illustrate, as well as descriptively detail, how sexism and racism often make this assumption inoperative. The promise of connectionalism versus congregationalism is that persons of color and women are more likely to receive at least beginning parish appointments. Election to the episcopacy or selection to national office can and does occur, but being appointed as senior minister at a large member high-steeple church eludes almost all except white males. The actual practical reach of "open itineracy" yet remains beyond the denomination's grasp.

The "generic vision of clergy appointable anywhere," claims sociologist Sally B. Geis, is dysfunctional in an inclusive church that embraces a pluralism of generational and class differences, rural and urban settings, life-styles and so forth. Rejecting prejudiced stereotypes and segregated systems, Geis contends clergy cannot be treated as a homogeneous group, any one of whom can be appointed to any congregation. Sometimes conference boundaries must be transcended in order to find the best possible person to fill a particular pulpit or to achieve a special missional task. Lyle Schaller also advocates abandoning this assumption, as he looks at the needs of large membership churches.

The "clergy appointable anywhere" assumption has also complicated the issue of whether openly gay and lesbian persons should serve as United Methodist clergy. A persuasive case might be made for appointing a gay or lesbian pastor to serve in a predominantly homosexual church and/or community. How fitting, for instance, has been Julian Rush's appointment beyond the local church to be Colorado AIDS Director during a time of great human crisis and need. However, the myth that each clergy must be appointable anywhere simply serves as another stumbling stone for the acceptance and affirmation of openly lesbian and gay persons in ministry.

Crossing cultural, racial, and gender boundaries generally remains an unfulfilled promise, yet this challenge pulls the church to a new vision of inclusiveness and opportunity. I affirm with Morrison and Caldwell that United Methodism is uniquely positioned to offer moral leadership to the world, but first "if we believe that God is calling us to cross all kinds of boundaries, then we must transcend our own boundaries."

Reassessing or revising these six assumptions or presuppositions will lead to other principles seemingly intrinsic to itineracy. Advocates of the *status quo* will argue that the boundaries and exceptions cannot be stretched any further. To do so would be to invite disaster. Architects of change, however, will point to evolutionary advances in the past and envision new structures and policies. Not to do so would be to solicit doom. Where do we go from here?

Revitalizing Itineracy for a Renewed Church

Strike up a conversation on itineracy with any United Methodist, lay or clergy, and discover that sparks begin to fly. Flames of opinion quickly rage as people share their viewpoints. One purpose of this book has been to help focus this debate, by clarifying past history and sharpening contemporary issues. Whether this dialogical exchange yields any permanent changes, depends on what people do to restructure policies and procedures in regard to clergy deployment.

In a Harvard University class on international politics, sociologist Seymour Lipset once remarked that all revolutions began with "students or drunks, because they had nothing to lose." Add "associate pastors" and you have a cadre for rebellion! In an early South Dakota pastorate I edited *The Plumb Line,* a journal that brazenly believed it possible to reform every conference institution and structure. Calling ourselves AMOS (Associated Ministries of Support), we associate pastors dared to ask questions and publicly discuss issues that senior colleagues feared to address. Having broken taboos, we suddenly found ourselves thrust into unexpected positions of leadership. We were challenged to develop new solutions to perplexing problems.

New alternatives for itineracy are unlikely to emerge from the episcopal hierarchy. As an old Irish proverb proclaims, reform always comes from the disadvantaged because the person with four aces never asks for a redeal. Seminary faculties are too immune from itineracy's ills to generate a flow of ideas for reforms. Likewise, waiting for national or even conference committees to consider this agenda may be an exercise in futility. Unless those who are hurting press for reformation, those who benefit from the system are unlikely to be catalysts for change. Clergy couples, note Kenneth L. Waters and Lydia J. Waters, understand this political phenomenon and attempt to actively influence church legislation and leadership. Others must also organize. Passive complaining yields little change; systematic and strategic plans to alter the system must materialize.

Not every new idea advanced for revitalizing itineracy will be received with favor. James O'Kelly discovered this truth in 1792.

Disgruntled with his appointment by Francis Asbury, he appealed to the conference. After listening to O'Kelly, the preachers rejected his arguments.

United Methodist mechanisms for change make extreme measures like clergy unions, spouse strikes, and congregational boycotts both unnecessary and unlikely. Any layperson or clergyperson can petition the General Conference and ask that disciplinary provisions be changed in a democratic fashion. An organization called MAIM (Methodists Against Itinerant Ministry) has been formed. Grassroots movements in any conference usually capture attention and specific proposals will be given due consideration. Laity and congregations can study the issues and state their cases. Retired and/or active clergy can share experiences and perspectives and shape creative new approaches.

A proposal envisioned by a South Indiana district superintendent, W. Robb Kell, illustrates the type of bold and innovative thinking needed for a revitalized itineracy in a renewed church. He has proposed a modified itineracy process that includes publicizing openings prompted by pastoral retirements or moves. The local pastor-parish relations committee would prepare a document evaluating their present situation, including their needs and salary range. This document would be circulated to all conference clergy. Those pastors interested would submit dossiers to their district superintendent. The bishop and cabinet would select three candidates from those interested and send their vitaes to the pastor-parish relations committee. The committee would request to interview one of the candidates, completing an evaluation form stating in detail reasons for accepting or rejecting the candidate. The bishop would then make an appointment on the basis of the cabinet's recommendation of the evaluations submitted by the committee. Kell believes these modifications, or similar changes, could be implemented without General Conference action.[34]

Experimenting with new approaches should be encouraged, lest rigor mortis characterizes United Methodism. Kell's proposals and others should be examined and critiqued. During a serendipitous moment of debate, the Holy Spirit may be heard. Persons unafraid of, or at least unencumbered by, ecclesiastical pressure or possible recrimination may be the stimulus needed to advance the caring and careful deployment of pastors for the kingdom of God.

Bishop Nolan Harmon liked to say that "we believe this plan to be providential; it has worked wonders, and we expect to adhere to it till the trump of judgment sounds."[35] The trumpet may now be blowing as membership and morale decline. Today few United Methodists believe that itineracy was in the "mind of God from the beginning," but affirm itineracy as a human invention that, in M. Kent Millard's language, God has marvelously used "to lead people to Christ and to serve the missional needs of the world." Just as the system has changed over the centuries to accommodate new contexts and circumstances, it can again be restructured to respect the dignity of all, yet advance the mission and ministry of the church in the world. As the distinguished Methodist church historian Frederick A. Norwood once wrote:

> It matters not what happens to the itineracy. . . . What really matters is that Methodists of our day recover the vision that has been ours from the beginning, accept the special call to a world parish without looking back, and understand, as Wesley wrote to Joseph Benson, "We are debtors to all the world."[36]

What needs to emerge is a re-visioned itineracy for a renewed church in the revitalized new world of the twenty-first century. When this happens, clergy will respond joyfully to the call for mission and ministry: "Send me."

NOTES

Whom Shall We Send?

1. *Daily Christian Advocate,* April 27, 1988, p. 82. The address was written and delivered by Bishop Jack M. Tuell of Los Angeles. Though not reflecting the view of every bishop at every point, in finished form this address was approved in advance by the Council of Bishops of The United Methodist Church.

2. *Daily Christian Advocate,* Advance Edition, pp. E-67-68

3. *Daily Christian Advocate,* April 27, 1988, p. 82.

4. Ibid.

5. This section and others in this introduction originated in initial discussions with A. James Armstrong and Sally B. Geis at The Iliff School of Theology, culminating in an essay entitled, "Revisioning Itineracy in The United Methodist Church" (Denver: Iliff Institute for Lay and Clergy Education, 1989). Since we wrote it together, revising draft after draft, it is now quite impossible to cite exactly who wrote particular paragraphs and sentences.

6. *Daily Christian Advocate,* April 27, 1988, p. 82.

1. Itineracy in Early Methodism

1. See Minton Thrift, *Memoir of the Rev. Jesse Lee. With Extracts from his Journals* (New York: N. Bangs and T. Mason for the Methodist Episcopal Church, 1823), p. 145.

2. *The Doctrines and Discipline of the Methodist Episcopal Church in America, With Explanatory Notes by Thomas Coke and Francis Asbury* (Philadelphia, 1798; Facsimile Edition, ed. Frederick A. Norwood, Rutland: Academy Books, 1979), p. 42.

3. And that notwithstanding the initiatory and critical role played by laity and lay preachers from the start and thereafter, a point made frequently and eloquently by Frederick Norwood. See his "The Americanization of the Wesleyan Itinerant," *The Ministry in the Methodist Heritage,* ed. Gerald O. McCulloh (Nashville: Department of Ministerial Education, 1960), pp. 33-66 and *The Story of American Methodism* (Nashville: Abingdon Press, 1974), especially pp. 61-69, "Lay Beginnings."

4. Edgar M. Bacon and Andrew C. Wheeler, *Nation Builders. A Story* (New York: Eaton & Mains, © 1905), pp. 20-21.

5. Robert Paine, *Life and Times of William McKendree,* 2 vols. (Nashville: Publishing House of the Methodist Episcopal Church, South, 1874), I, p. 115. Concurring that "our plan is Providential" was the author of *The Bishop's Council: With Reminiscences of an Annual Conference of the Methodist Episcopal Church by an Ex-Presiding Elder* (Saint Louis: P.M. Pinckard, 1867), p. 16.

6. "There is no feature of our economy more highly prized among us than its *itinerancy.* It is believed by many that much of our extraordinary success in saving souls is attributable to this peculiarity of Wesleyanism, more than to any other one thing." James Porter, *The Revised Compendium of Methodism* (New York: Hunt & Eaton, 1875), p. 350.

7. Gerald Kennedy, "The Genius of the Methodist Itinerancy," *Forever Beginning, 1766–1966,* ed. Albea Godbold (Lake Junaluska: Commission on Archives and History, 1968), p. 195.

8. *The Methodist Magazine,* XXV (1843):278, quoted by James David Lynn in *The Concept of the Ministry in the Methodist Episcopal Church, 1784–1844* (Princeton Theological Seminary, Ph.Diss., 1973), p. 223.

9. *Minutes of the Methodist Conferences Annually Held in America: From 1773 to 1813, Inclusive* (New York: 1813; Reprint ed. Swainsboro, Ga.: Magnolia Press, 1983), 6, (Minutes, 1773).

10. Other contextual constellations vital for understanding itinerancy but impossible to cover here are (5) the range of ministerial tasks deemed vital for the church and society of the day and the priorities established among them; (6) the procedures for selection, preparation and nurture of the preachers, including both the Course of Study and theological education; (7) the theology of church and ministry, both explicit and implicit, in terms of which itinerancy was both understood and exercised. On the latter, see Thomas A. Langford, *Practical Divinity* (Nashville: Abingdon, 1983); Dow Kirkpatrick, ed., *The Doctrine of the Church* (New York: Abingdon, 1964); Dennis M. Campbell, *The Yoke of Obedience* (Nashville: Abingdon, 1988); Leon O. Hynson, *To Reform the Nation* (Grand Rapids: Francis Asbury, 1984); and M. Douglas Meeks, ed., *The Future of the Methodist Theological Traditions* (Nashville: Abingdon, 1985). For (6), see Gerald O. McCulloh, *Ministerial Education in the American Methodist Movement* (Nashville: United Methodist Board of Higher Education and Ministry, 1980).

11. For suggestive treatment of how the Awakening and Whitefield revolutionized American rhetoric, see Harry S. Stout, *The New England Soul: Preaching and Religious Culture in Colonial New England* (New York: Oxford University Press, 1986).

12. See Russell E. Richey, "The Southern Accent of American Methodism," *Methodist History,* XXVII (October 1988): 3-24.

13. So we see in the work of Charles Woodmason, the South Carolina Anglican itinerant in Richard J. Hooker, ed., *The Carolina Backcountry on the Eve of the Revolution. The Journal and Other Writings of Charles Woodmason, Anglican Itinerant* (Chapel Hill: University of North Carolina Press, 1953).

14. See F. Ernest Stoeffler, ed., *Continental Pietism and Early American Christianity* (Grand Rapids: William B. Eerdmans, 1976).

15. J. Bruce Behney and Paul H. Eller, *The History of the Evangelical United Brethren Church,* ed. Kenneth W. Krueger (Nashville: Abingdon, 1979), pp. 31-45, 52.

16. The former connection has been brilliantly traced by E. Brooks Holifield in *A History of Pastoral Care in America* (Nashville: Abingdon Press, 1983).

17. See Russell E. Richey, "Evolving Patterns of Methodist Ministry," *Methodist History,* XXII (October 1983): 20-37.

18. Frederick A. Norwood, "The Americanization of the Wesleyan Itinerant," and Luther W. King, *An Historical Study of Ministerial Authority in American Methodism: 1760 to 1940* (Columbia University, Ph.D.diss., 1981).

19. Nathan O. Hatch, *The Democratization of American Christianity* (New Haven: Yale University Press, 1989). For an illustration of Methodist evaluation of itinerancy's cultural impact, see Nathan Bangs, *A History of the Methodist Episcopal Church,* 12th ed., 4 vols. (New York: Carlton & Porter, 1860), I, pp. 362-63.

20. Daniel H. Calhoon, *Professional Lives in America* (Cambridge: Harvard University Press, 1965). Sidney E. Mead, "The Rise of the Evangelical Conception of the Ministry in America (1607–1850)," *The Ministry in Historical Perspectives,* ed. by H. Richard Niebuhr and Daniel D. Williams (San Francisco: Harper & Row, 1956, 1963), pp. 207-49.

21. Campbell, *The Yoke of Obedience,* pp. 47-68.

22. Albert C. Outler, ed., *The Works of John Wesley, Sermons,* IV (Nashville: Abingdon Press, 1984), pp. 79-80.

23. Parallel presentation of the 1780 *Large Minutes* and the first American *Discipline* can be found in Appendix VII of Jno. J. Tigert, *A Constitutional History of American Episcopal Methodism,* 3rd ed. (Nashville: Publishing House of the Methodist Episcopal Church, South, 1908) and p. 550 for the items cited. See also *The Works of John Wesley,* (Jackson edition, Grand Rapids: Zondervan, reprint of 1872 edition), VIII, 309. The 12th Rule of a Helper is worth particular note:

> Act in all Things, not according to your own Will, but as a Son in the Gospel. As such it is your Part to employ your Time in the Manner which we direct: Partly in Preaching and visiting from House to House: Partly in Reading, Meditation, and Prayer. Above all, if you labour with us in our Lord's Vineyard, it is needful you should do *that Part* of the Work which we advise, at *those Times and Places* which we judge most for his Glory.

This stylizing of the Rule is from the first *Discipline.*

24. One gets a sense of that process by following the legislative additions to the *Discipline.* See for instance, Robert Emory, *History of The Discipline of the Methodist Episcopal Church,* rev. by W. P. Strickland (New York: Carlton & Porter, © 1856) which itemizes changes by *Disciplinary* paragraph. Note especially pp. 152-206.

25. See Behney and Eller, *History,* pp. 114-17 and pp. 131-33.

26. J. Manning Potts, ed. *The Journal and Letters of Francis Asbury,* ed., 3 vols. (London: Epworth Press and Nashville: Abingdon Press, 1958), III, pp. 491-92 [hereinafter JLFA].

27. C. C. Goss, *Statistical History of the First Century of American Methodism: With a Summary of the Origin and Present Operations of Other Denominations* (New York: Carlton & Porter, 1866), pp. 168-70.

28. Minton Thrift, *Memoir of the Rev. Jesse Lee. With Extracts from his Journals* (New York: N. Bangs and T. Mason for the Methodist Episcopal Church, 1823), p. 42.

29. "The United Methodist System of Itinerant Ministry," p. 18.

30. *Doctrines and Discipline,* 1798, p. 34.

31. And fittingly constituted themselves with a *Discipline.*

32. Mudge, *New England Conference,* pp. 66, 98. Compare William Warren Sweet,

ed., *The Rise of Methodism in the West, Being the Journal of the Western Conference 1800–1811* (New York and Cincinnati: The Methodist Book Concern, 1920), 100-109.

33. "Autobiography of Rev. William Burke," in James B. Finley, *Sketches of Western Methodism: Biographical, Historical, and Miscellaneous,* ed. W. P. Strickland (Cincinnati: Methodist Book Concern, 1854), p. 27.

34. The flavor of conference and its fraternal character is summarized by James Mudge, *History of the New England Conference of the Methodist Episcopal Church, 1796–1910* (Boston: Published for the Conference, 1910) in a section entitled "Life in the Conference," pp. 177-208. See pp. 177-78 on conference's gathering.

35. Will B. Gravely, "African Methodism and the Rise of Black Denominationalism," *Rethinking Methodist History,* pp. 111-24. Hillah F. Thomas, Rosemary Skinner Keller, and Louise L. Queen, eds., *Women in New Worlds* 2 vols. (Nashville: Abingdon, 1981, 1982), especially I: Rosemary Skinner Keller, "Creating a Sphere for Women: The Methodist Episcopal Church, 1869–1906" and the four essays in II, section IV.

36. See the forthcoming volume by Jean Miller Schmidt, *Grace Sufficient.*

37. *Sketches of The Life and Travel of Rev. Thomas Ware* (New York: G. Land & P. P. Sandford, 1842). Most major figures enjoyed national careers like that of Ware. One of the most celebrated was Martin Ruter whose career went from New England to Texas (Bangs, *History,* IV, pp. 288-91; Mudge, *New England Conference,* p. 76). Less prominent ministers also labored nationally. Finley, *Sketches,* 185-89. Compare "A Sketch of the Labours and Travels of Ira Ellis," JLFA, II, pp. 460-61.

38. JLFA, III, p. 475.

39. C. C. Goen, *Broken Churches, Broken Nation. Denominational Schisms and the Coming of the American Civil War* (Macon: Mercer University Press, 1985). A contemporary perspective comes from Jacob Lanius in Elmer T. Clark, ed., *The Journal of The Reverend Jacob Lanius* (1918), pp. 237-38.

40. The office is recognized in the 1789 *Discipline.*

41. The evolution of the office from an ordinary to an extraordinary one, the addition of appointive to its sacramental functions, is most clearly seen in the successive disciplinary legislation in Emory, *History of the Discipline,* pp. 136 ff.

42. *Discipline,* 1792 in Emory, p. 138.

43. *Discipline,* 1786; Emory, p. 137.

44. One of several quarterly meetings on Redstone circuit detailed by Robert Ayres, *Mss. Journal,* cited by Wallace G. Smeltzer in *Methodism on the Headwaters of the Ohio* (Nashville: The Parthenon Press, 1951), pp. 61-62.

45. Nathan Bangs, *A History of the Methodist Episcopal Church,* 8th ed., 4 vols. (New York: Carlton & Porter, 1860), III, p. 304.

46. Emory, *History of the Discipline,* pp. 191-202.

47. Mudge noted:

> The locations from the breaking down of health or from family necessities, and the early deaths, were incessant and ruinous to the work. Of 600 who belonged to the itinerant ministry prior to 1800, about 500 located permanently, besides very many who, after an interval, reentered the traveling connection. Of the fifty-five young men who entered the New York Conference in 1801, twenty-nine retired from the ministry within the short period of ten years. During the first fifty years more than half of all who entered the ministry were obliged to locate. During the quadrennium ending in 1840 the locations reached 546, or more than one-fourth of the whole number in the itinerant ranks at its commencement.

He continued, "The places of those who retired, often men of cultivated talent and experience, had to be supplied with ever fresh drafts of untried men, a portentous evil. . . ." James Mudge, *History of the New England Conference of the Methodist Episcopal Church, 1796–1910,* p. 110.

48. JLFA, II, p. 474, July 9, 1805. Asbury's sentiments prevailed within the traveling ranks as this comment by Finley concerning Benjamin Lakin's 1797 marriage indicates:

> Such was the prejudice that existed in the Church, at that day, against married preachers, that it was almost out of the question for any man to continue in the work if he had a wife. They were not exactly obliged to take the Popish vow of celibacy, but it almost amounted to the same thing; and there being such a high example for single life, as exhibited in the cases of the bishops, if a preacher married he was looked upon almost as a heretic who had denied the faith. Besides, no provision was made for the wife, and she was regarded, on all hands, as an incumbrance. Finley, *Sketches,* pp. 180-81.

Preachers nevertheless married and located. The continuing seriousness of this prompted a study and report at the 1816 General Conference by the Committee of Ways and Means on the loss to church through locations of its experienced, trained, and pious "ornaments." *Journals of the General Conference of The Methodist Episcopal Church,* I, 1796–1836 (New York: Carlton & Phillips, 1855), pp. 148-52.

49. Lee, *Short History of the Methodists,* p. 255.

50. *History of the New England Conference of the Methodist Episcopal Church, 1796–1910,* pp. 239-40. Mudge observed:

> The lay or local preachers and exhorters have formed, from the beginning, a very important factor in the work. The great extent of the early circuits would of itself imply this. . . . We have no way of ascertaining accurately the number of these early local preachers, for the statistics of the Minutes do not recognize them till 1837, when the number in the whole church is given as 4,954 as against 2,933 in the itinerant ranks. Only eighty-five are reported at that time from the New England Conference, or about half the number of those traveling. In 1850 the local preachers of this Conference were eighty as compared with 113 traveling, and in the whole church 5,420 as compared with 3,777. In 1870 there were 10,340 local, and 8,830 traveling. In 1890 the numbers were practically equal, 14,072 local and 14,792 traveling. At present there are 14,743 local and 19,421 traveling.

51. Ibid., p. 241.

52. Frederick A. Norwood, *The Story of American Methodism* (Nashville: Abingdon Press, 1974), p. 132. See the pages following for Norwood's discussion of the local ministry.

53. *Minutes . . . 1773 to 1813, Inclusive,* pp. 8, 147.

54. See Dunlap, "The United Methodist System of Itinerant Ministry," pp. 23-26.

55. *The Book of Discipline of The United Methodist Church,* 1988 (Nashville: United Methodist Publishing House, 1988), pp. 80-84, 7-18, 40-60. See Russell E. Richey, "The Role of History in The Discipline," *Quarterly Review* 10 (Winter 1989), : 3-20.

2. When Korea Abolished Guaranteed Appointments

1. Richard B. Wilke, *And Are We Yet Alive?* (Nashville: Abingdon Press, 1986), pp. 10-16. See also Carl S. Dudley, *Where Have All Our People Gone?* (New York: The Pilgrim Press, 1979), pp. 4-6.

2. *The Great Christian Manuals* (Seoul: Kyomun Sa, 1986), pp. 662-63.

Presbyterianism in Korea split into sixty or more divisions in spite of great numerical growth. Korean Methodism preserves its unity even with comparatively slow growth.

3. *The Book of Discipline* (Nashville: The United Methodist Publishing House, 1984), p. 9.

4. Ibid.

5. C. A. Sauer, *Methodist in Korea* (Seoul: The Christian Literature Society, 1973), p. 27.

6. Ibid.

7. Ibid., pp. 105-9.

8. Ibid., p. 149.

9. Kwang Woo Kim, ed., *One Hundred Years of Korean Methodist Church* (Seoul: Jeon Mang Sa, 1990), p. 419.

10. *The Great Christian Manuals,* 1986 ed., pp. 661-63; 1988 ed., p. 585.

11. *Resource Book,* Korean Methodist Church Planning Committee for the Celebration of the 60th Anniversary of Autonomy, 1990, p. 29.

12. James W. Holsinger, Jr., and Evelyn Laycock, *Awaken the Giant* (Nashville: Abingdon Press, 1989), p. 137.

13. Wilke, *And Are We Yet Alive?,* pp. 102-3.

14. Ibid.

15. Ernst Troeltsch, *The Social Teachings of the Christian Churches,* Vol. II (New York and Evanston: Harper & Bros., 1931), p. 461.

16. *The Book of Discipline,* p. 9.

17. Colin W. Williams, *John Wesley's Theology Today* (New York and Nashville: Abingdon Press, 1960), p. 149.

18. Robert A. Evans, "Recovering the Church's Transforming Middle," in *Understanding Church Growth and Decline: 1950–1978,* ed. Dean R. Hoge and David A. Roozen (New York and Philadelphia: The Pilgrim Press, 1979), p. 312.

3. *Without Reserve: A Critical Appreciation of Itineracy*

1. Nathan Mitchell, *History and Theology in the Sacrament of Order* (Wilmington, Del.: Mihael Glazier, 1982), p. 15.

2. The most thorough defense of itineracy as biblically based was written by Able Stevens in his *Essay of Church Polity* in 1847. A summary of this essay can be found in an unpublished paper by E. Dale Dunlap, retired academic dean of Saint Paul School of Theology. An edited version of the Dunlap paper is found in Russell E. Richey and Kenneth E. Rowe, ed., *Rethinking Methodist History: A Bicentennial Historical Consultation* (Nashville: Kingswood Books, 1985).

3. The three lay preachers were Thomas Maxfield, Thomas Richards, and Thomas Westall. See Henry D. Rack, *Reasonable Enthusiast* (Philadelphia: Trinity Press International, 1989), pp. 210ff.

4. Ibid.

5. Ibid., p. 211.

6. Ibid., p. 247.

7. Ibid., p. 249.

8. Ibid., p. 287.

9. Ibid., p. 249.

10. Charles W. Ferguson, *Organizing to Beat the Devil: Methodists and the Making of America* (New York: Doubleday, 1971), p. 109.

11. Richey and Rowe, *Rethinking Methodist History,* p. 11.
12. From an address printed by the Lilly Endowment Project on Ministerial Recruitment.
13. A phrase used by Bishop Joseph H. Yeakel in *The Circuit Rider* (July-August 1978), p. 16. Also see chapter 2 in Bishop R. Sheldon Duecker, *Tensions in the Connection* (Nashville: Abingdon Press, 1983).
14. "The Ministerial Covenant in The United Methodist Church Today, *Quarterly Review,* vol. 10, no. 1 (Spring 1990):30.
15. William Willimon, *Rekindling the Flame* (Nashville: Abingdon Press, 1987), p. 48.
16. Ibid., p. 51.
17. Some guidelines for consultation are found in Earl G. Hunt, *A Bishop Speaks His Mind* (Nashville: Abingdon Press, 1987), pp. 72-73.
18. Edward Schillebeeckx, *Ministry: Leadership in the Community* (New York: Crossroad Publishing Co., 1981).
19. Ibid., p. 105.
20. Ibid., p. 128.
21. Dennis Campbell, *The Yoke of Obedience: The Meaning of Ordination in Methodism* (Nashville: Abingdon Press, 1988), pp. 102-3.
22. This point is stated clearly and concisely by Donald E. Messer, *Contemporary Images of Christian Ministry* (Nashville: Abingdon Press, 1989), p. 147.
23. See James K. Mathews, *Set Apart to Serve: The Role of the Episcopacy in the Wesleyan Tradition* (Nashville: Abingdon Press, 1985), pp. 203-4.
24. *The Christian Century,* 107, no. 25 (September 5-12, 1990).
25. Quoted in Robert Moats Miller, *Bishop G. Bromley Oxnam: Paladin of Liberal Protestantism* (Nashville: Abingdon Press, 1990), p. 320.
26. Hunt, *A Bishop Speaks His Mind,* p. 72.
27. *Quarterly Review* (Spring 1990): 33.

4. Spiritual Discernment in Consultation

1. Steve Harper, *John Wesley's Message for Today* (Grand Rapids, Michigan: Francis Asbury Press, 1983), p. 18.
2. John Wesley, *The Letters of the Rev. John Wesley,* ed. John Telford, vol. 4 (London: Epworth, 1960), p. 103.
3. John Wesley, *The Works of the Rev. John Wesley, M.A.*, ed. Thomas Jackson, vol. VIII (London, John Mason, 1829), p. 311.
4. Frank Baker, *John Wesley of the Church of England* (Nashville: Abingdon Press, 1970), p. 17.
5. Horace Greeley Smith, "The Itinerant Ministry," in *Methodism,* ed. William K. Anderson (Cincinnati: The Methodist Publishing House, 1947), p. 169.
6. *The Book of Discipline of The United Methodist Church* (Nashville: The United Methodist Publishing House, 1988), p. 293.
7. Danny Morris, "Spiritual Discernment" (Unpublished paper presented at Fort Worth Convention Center, October 31, 1990), Fort Worth, Texas, p. 3.
8. Douglas V. Steere, "Some Dimensions of the Quaker Decision Making Process," *Friends Journal* (May 15, 1982):20.

5. Reaffirming the Covenant in Itineracy

1. Bishop Jack M. Tuell, "The Episcopal Address," *Daily Christian Advocate,* 1988 General Conference, April 27, 1988, p. 82.
2. Quoted by E. Dale Dunlap, "The System of Itineracy in American Methodism," an essay for the Division of Ordained Ministry, Nashville, 1978, p. 19.
3. Dunlap, "System of Itineracy," p. 7.
4. *The Book of Discipline,* 1988, Par. 112.4.
5. Ibid., Par. 422.
6. Nolan B. Harmon, *History of American Methodism,* Vol. III, ed. E. S. Burke (New York: Abingdon Press, 1964), p. 21.
7. Dunlap, "System of Itineracy," p. 33.
8. *The Book of Discipline,* Par. 520.1.
9. Tuell, "The Episcopal Address," p. 82.
10. Michael G. Nickerson, researcher, *Survey of Appointment Tenure for Ordained Elders* (Nashville: Division of Ordained Ministry, 1989).
11. Tuell, "The Episcopal Address," p. 82.
12. Dunlap, "System of Itineracy," p. 1.
13. J. T. Crane, "Our Itineracy," *Methodist Quarterly Review* (January 1866) : 73.
14. Dunlap, "System of Itineracy," p. 2.
15. Horace Greeley Smith, "The Itinerant Ministry," in *Methodism,* ed. William K. Anderson (Cincinnati: Methodist Publishing House, 1947), p. 165.
16. *The Book of Discipline,* Par. 423.2.
17. *The Book of Discipline,* Par. 453.3.
18. Tuell, "The Episcopal Address," p. 82.

6. Who Is the Client? The Clergy or the Congregation?

1. Donald M. Scott, *From Office to Profession* (Philadelphia: University of Pennsylvania Press, 1978), p. 4.
2. Douglas Johnson, "Small Membership Churches," *Background Data for Mission* (New York: Research Office, National Program Division, General Board of Global Ministries, September, 1990).
3. It may be totally unrealistic to expect an annual conference, where authority is broadly dispersed among many boards, committees, and the cabinet to be able to prepare a strategic plan. For a provocative discussion on this point see Richard A. Gabriel, *Military Incompetence* (New York: The Noonday Press, 1985), pp. 5-27.

7. A Generic Lay Perspective

1. *InfoServe,* A service of United Methodist Communications. Telephone conversation, October 26, 1990.
2. Tex Sample, *U.S. Lifestyles and Mainline Churches* (Westminster: John Knox Press, 1990), pp. 5, 17-19.
3. Wade Clark Roof and William McKinney, *American Mainline Religion* (New Brunswick: Rutgers University Press, 1987), p. 17.
4. Ibid.
5. Board of Higher Education and Ministry, Nashville, TN. Telephone conversation, October 26, 1990.

6. Sample, *U.S. Lifestyles and Mainline Churches,* p. 11.
7. Ibid., p. 17.
8. Ibid., p. 16.
9. James W. Holsinger, Jr. and Evelyn Laycock, *Awakening the Giant* (Nashville: Abingdon Press, 1989), pp. 29-42.
10. Report by the Planning and Research Committee of the Rocky Mountain Conference Council on Ministries, Walter Boigegrain, Chairperson, Unpublished paper, June, 1990.
11. Ross Kinsler, Seminario Biblico Latinoamericano, San Jose, Costa Rica. See also R. Sheldon Duecker, *Tensions in the Connection* (Nashville: Abingdon Press, 1983); Richard B. Wilke, *And Are We Yet Alive: The Future of the United Methodist Church* (Nashville: Abingdon Press, 1986); Jack Tuell, Episcopal Address, General Conference 1988, as printed in *The Daily Christian Advocate* (April 27, 1988): 82; and William H. Willimon and Robert L. Wilson, *Rekindling the Flame* (Nashville: Abingdon Press, 1987).
12. Donald E. Messer, *Contemporary Images of Christian Ministry* (Nashville: Abingdon Press, 1989), p. 77.
13. Ibid., p. 76.
14. Andrew Abbott, *The System of Professions: An Essay on the Division of Expert Labor* (Chicago: University of Chicago Press, 1988), pp. 19-20.
15. Ibid., pp. 186-87.
16. Ibid., p. 170.
17. Rebecca S. Chopp, "A Model of Ministry for Theological Education," *Criterion* (August 1982): 9.
18. Private conversation with Mortimer Arias at The Iliff School of Theology, Denver, Colorado, October, 1990.
19. Lynn N. Rhodes, *Co-Creating a Feminist Vision of Ministry* (Philadelphia: The Westminster Press, 1987), pp. 17-18.
20. *The New York Times* (January 28, 1990), p. 24.
21. Don Donato, "Council of Bishops Renews Anti-Drug Effort" *The United Methodist Reporter* (November 16, 1990), p. 1.
22. Bishop Felton May, *The New York Times* (January 28, 1990), p. 24.
23. *The Washington Post* (Saturday, June 2, 1990), p. B1. See also *The Los Angeles Times* (Friday, July 6, 1990), pp. 1, 9, and *The Rocky Mountain News* (Saturday, October 20, 1990), p. 30.
24. Messer, *Contemporary Images of Christian Ministry,* pp. 97-115.

8. *Crossing Cultural, Racial, and Gender Boundaries*

1. Church historian Jean Miller Schmidt at The Iliff School of Theology notes that the Methodist Episcopal Church granted limited clergy rights ("partial status") to women in 1924; that is, they could be ordained local deacon or local elder. Not until 1956 were women made part of the itinerant ministry—given full clergy rights with Annual Conference membership—in The United Methodist Church. Of the predecessor bodies of what is now The United Methodist Church, the Methodist Protestant Church and the United Brethren were first to ordain women, beginning in the 1880s and 1890s.
2. Rosemary Radford Ruether, *Disputed Questions: On Being a Christian,* ed. Robert A. Raines (Nashville: Abingdon Press, 1982), p. 141.

3. Sydney S. Sadio, *Open Itineracy in The United Methodist Church* (Princeton: Princeton University Press, 1984), pp. 78-79.

4. George E. Schreckengost, "The Effect of Latent Racist, Ethnic, and Sexual Biases on Placement," *Review of Religious Research*, vol. 28, no. 4 (June 1987), p. 351.

5. Donald E. Messer, *Contemporary Images of Christian Ministry* (Nashville: Abingdon Press, 1989), pp. 49-50.

6. Prathia Hall Wynn, foreword to *Those Preachin' Women: Sermons by Black Women Preachers*, Ella Pearson Mitchel, ed. (Valley Forge, Pa.: Judson Press, 1985), p. 9.

9. Conflicting Covenants: Clergy Spouses and Families

1. "Address of the Bishops," in *Journal of the General Conference of the Methodist Episcopal Church, Held in the City of New York, 1884* (New York: Carlton and Phillips, 1856), pp. 158-60; quoted in Leonard I. Sweet, *The Minister's Wife: Her Role in Nineteenth-Century American Evangelicalism* (Philadelphia: Temple University Press, 1983), p. 49.

2. Frederick A. Norwood, "The Church Takes Shape," in *The History of American Methodism*, vol. I, ed. Emory Stevens Bucke (Nashville: Abingdon Press, 1964), p. 469.

3. Ibid.

4. *Itinerant Preaching in the Early Days of Methodism by a Pioneer Preacher's Wife*, Mrs. Mary Orne Tucker, edited by her son, Thomas W. Tucker (Boston: B. B. Russel, 1872), p. 57 in *The Nineteenth-Century American Methodist Itinerant Preacher's Wife*, edited with an introduction by Carolyn DeSwarte Giffort (New York: Garland Publishing, 1987).

5. Ibid., p. 77.

6. Herrick M. Eaton, *The Itinerant's Wife: Her Qualification, Duties, Trials and Rewards* (New York: Lane & Scott, 1851), p. 55, in Gifford, *The Nineteenth-Century American Methodist Itinerant Preacher's Wife.*

7. G. Lloyd Rediger, "Revolution in the Parsonage," *The Christian Ministry* (January 1986), p. 5.

8. William Douglas, *Ministers' Wives* (New York: Harper & Row, 1965), p. 32.

9. George L. Proctor-Smith, "Is There (Married) Life After Itineracy?" *Circuit Rider* (November/December 1986), p. 11.

10. Rediger, "Revolution in the Parsonage," p. 7.

11. "Memphis Conference Studies Clergy Morale," *Facts and Figures* (Nashville: Office of Research, General Conference on Ministries of The United Methodist Church, March 1987), p. 2.

12. Anita J. Herrick and Dee Ann Mezger, *The Circuit Rider* (September 1982), p. 6.

13. Eaton, *The Itinerant's Wife*, p. 68.

14. Audrey T. McCollum, *The Trauma of Moving*, Vol. 182 (Newbury Park, Calif.: Sage Library of Social Research, 1990), p. 12.

15. For a discussion of the correlates of depression, see Aaron T. Beck, et al., *Cognitive Therapy of Depression* (New York: Guilford Press, 1979).

16. McCollum, *The Trauma of Moving*, p. 85.

17. *Daily Christian Advocate*, April 27, 1988, p. 82.

18. James F. Childress and John Macquarrie, eds., *The Westminster Dictionary of Christian Ethics* (Philadelphia: The Westminster Press, 1986), p. 136.

19. Ibid.

20. Margaret A. Farley, *Making, Keeping, and Breaking Personal Commitments* (San Francisco: Harper & Row, 1989), p. 59.

21. Laura Deming and Jack Stubbs, *Men Married to Ministers* (Alban Institute, 1986), p. 19.

10. Married to the Church and to Each Other: Clergy Couples

1. These figures were compiled by Tom and Sharon Neufer Emswiler in *Clergy Couples Connect* (May-June 1988):1. If all elders, deacons, and lay pastors were reported, the numbers could be close to 1,000 couples; 90 percent of this number are projected as ordained couples.

2. See Ronald A. Houk, "Let There Be Justice: But Whose Justice?" *Circuit Rider* (October 1988): 6-7, in response to Duane R. Miller, "Clergy Couples Bring a Time for Change in Our Itineracy," pp. 4-6. Miller's call for reform of the itineracy system and his comparison between clergy couples and clergy with "working lay spouses" have been particularly informative.

3. See memorandum No. 588 in "Decisions of the Judicial Council of The United Methodist Church" in *The 1988 General Minutes of the Annual Conference of The United Methodist Church* (Illinois: The General Council of Finance and Administration, 1988), pp. 1152-54. The position of the Judicial Council is that the issue hinges on a definition of "adequate housing." It is housing and not compensation that is to be provided under Par. 256.3(f). Therefore, if a clergy couple can be satisfactorily housed in the parsonage provided by one of the appointments, then the Annual Conference and the local church(s) have made "adequate provision." The Council is "unconvinced" by the contention that Par. 256.3(f) is discriminatory against clergy couples. Instead, "Additional housing allowance, unless provided as additional compensation after negotiation, would then be reverse discrimination of the minister who is not married to a clergy spouse." In decision 547 (October 1984) the Council emphasized that "there is nothing . . . to indicate that ministers may not negotiate for more compensation if they are not going to use the housing." The Council adds, however, "that the result of such negotiations is compensation and not housing."

A brief challenging the judicial council decisions has been prepared by Jerry Eckert. A version of the presentation appears as a five-part series, "The Housing Issue and Clergy Couples: Is Paragraph 256.3(f) Constitutional" in *Clergy Couples Connect* (January-February 1989) to (September-October 1989). Eckert's observations concerning the possible involvement of "institutional protectionism" helps expose some of the subtleties of this issue.

4. These gains in the areas of pensions and death benefits were brought to our attention by Tom and Sharon Neufer Emswiler in a brochure on clergy couples prepared by them for distribution through the Board of Higher Education and Ministry of The United Methodist Church.

5. These issues involving less than full-time service, hospitalization, and co-pastoring were brought to our attention by Doug and Sandy Essinger-Hileman in "General Conference Actions Related to Clergy Couples," *Clergy Couples Connect* (May-June 1988): 2, and "Time to Take Stock of United Methodist Gains and Losses," *Clergy Couples Connect* (September-October 1988):4.

6. What we mean by "broken" personalities can be ascertained from reading Kenneth C. Haugk's *Antagonists in the Church: How to Identify and Deal With Destructive Conflict* (Minneapolis: Augsburg Publishing House, 1988). Haugk, of

course, uses the term "antagonists" and not "broken personalities." We use the latter term to indicate the psychologically shattering effects that racism has had upon many people in global ethnic congregations—effects that can make pastoral leadership in such congregations especially difficult.

11. Liberation for a Culture in Crisis

1. I use the term liberation theology as the structuring horizon for the theological perspectives of women, blacks, Latin Americans, and others concerned with the prophetic critique of injustice, the transforming praxis of Christianity, and the spirituality of diverse voices. For further elaboration on my own perspectives, see Rebecca S. Chopp, *The Praxis of Suffering: An Interpretation of Liberation and Political Theology* (Maryknoll: Orbis Press, 1986), and *The Power to Speak: Feminism, Language, God* (New York: Crossroads, 1989).

2. See E. Dale Dunlap, "The System of Itineracy in American Methodism: An Historical Essay," (unpublished paper).

3. Nehemiah Curnock, ed., *The Journal of the Rev. John Wesley, A.M.* Vol. VII (London: Robert Culley, 1910), p. 422. (Quoted also in Dunlap, "The System of Itineracy").

4. In addition to the Dunlap article, for resources to begin reading on the history of itineracy, see Frank Baker, *From Wesley to Asbury: Studies in Early American Methodism* (Durham: Duke University Press, 1976); James David Lynn, *The Concept of Ministry in the Methodist Episcopal Church, 1784–1844* (Ann Arbor: University Microfilms, 1973); Frederick A. Norwood, *The Story of American Methodism* (Nashville: Abingdon Press, 1974); and, of course, *The History of American Methodism* (New York: Abingdon Press, 1964).

5. See Jürgen Moltmann, *Theology of Hope: On the Grounds and Implications of a Christian Eschatology* (San Francisco: Harper & Row, 1967).

6. See Robert N. Bellah, Richard Madsen, William M. Sullivan, Ann Swidler, and Steven M. Tipton, *Habits of the Heart: Individualism and Commitment in American Life* (New York: Harper & Row, 1985).

7. See, for instance, Augustine, *Confessions,* translated with an introduction by R. S. Pine-Coffin (London: Penguin Books, 1961, 1986).

8. See Johann Baptist Metz, *The Emergent Church: The Future of Christianity in a Postbourgeois World,* trans. Peter Mann (New York: Crossroad, 1981).

Where Do We Go From Here?

1. Martin Luther King, Jr. *Where Do We Go from Here: Chaos or Community?* (Boston: Beacon Press, 1967), p. 191.

2. Memorandum to the author from Roy I. Sano, December 14, 1990.

3. See my book, *Contemporary Images of Christian Ministry* (Nashville: Abingdon Press, 1989), pp. 24-25 and 37.

4. Donald E. Byrne, Jr., *No Foot of Land: Folklore of American Methodist Itinerants* (Metuchen: N.J.: Scarecrow Press, 1975), p. 270.

5. See William K. Anderson, ed., *Methodism* (Kansas City: The Methodist Publishing House, 1947), p. 167.

6. Robert T. Handy, "American Methodism and Its Historical Frontier: Interpret-

ing Methodism on the Western Frontier: Between Romanticism and Realism," *Methodist History* (October 1984): 48-49.

7. See William K. Anderson, ed., *Methodism* (Kansas City: The Methodist Publishing House, 1947), p. 167.

8. As quoted by L. C. Rudolph, *Francis Asbury* (Nashville: Abingdon Press, 1966), pp. 170-71.

9. See Frederick A. Norwood, "The Americanization of the Wesleyan Itinerant," *In the Ministry in the Methodist Heritage,* ed. Gerald O. McCulloh (Nashville: The Board of Education of the Methodist Church, 1960), p. 42, and Bruce D. Forbes, "Methodist Mission Among the Dakotas: A Case Study of Difficulties," in *Rethinking Methodist History: A Bicentennial Historical Consultation,* ed. Russell E. Richey and Kenneth E. Rowe (Nashville: Kingswood Books, 1985), p. 56.

10. See Jacob Young, *Autobiography of a Pioneer* (Cincinnati, 1857), p. 149. Also William K. Anderson, ed., *Methodism* (Kansas City: The Methodist Publishing House, 1947), pp. 169-70.

11. Historian W. W. Sweet in *The Methodists, Religion on the American Frontier,* 1783–1840, Vol. IV, p. 50, summarized the seriousness of the situation when he noted that: "The great loss of traveling ministers through their 'location' is shown by the fact that, of the 1,616 preachers received into the conferences from the beginning of American Methodism to 1814, 821 had located, most of them within a relatively few years after their admission; 131 had died in the service; 34 had been expelled; and 25 had withdrawn."

12. See Frederick A. Norwood, "The Americanization of the Wesleyan Itinerant," p. 35.

13. Michael G. Nickerson, "Historical Relationships of Itineracy and Salary," *Methodist History,* 21 (October 1982): 54-56.

14. See Stanley J. Menking, "The Itineracy Matures," *Circuit Rider* (February 1958): 4-5.

15. Russell E. Richey, "Evolving Patterns of Methodist Ministry," *Methodist History,* 22 (October 1983): 21.

16. Elijah Hedding, *A Discourse on the Administration of Discipline* (appended to the *Discipline,* 1842), p. 75.

17. Episcopal Address, 1912 (pamphlet edition), pp. 16 and 20.

18. George Bernard Shaw, *The Doctor's Dilemma: A Tragedy* (New York: The Trow Press, 1911), p. xv.

19. See James R. Crook, Jr., "Building Understanding Between the Pastor-Parish Relations Committee and the District Superintendent Concerning Consultation in Appointments in The United Methodist Church," D.Min. Project, Drew University, 1987.

20. James R. Crook, Jr., "Building Understanding," p. 78.

21. Don W. Holter, "Some Changes Related To The Ordained Ministry In The History of American Methodism," *Methodist History/A.M.E. Zion,* p. 180.

22. See *Newscope,* September 28, 1990, p. 2.

23. Greater research is required to document this perception. Disputing this assertion, Michael G. Nickerson in "Historical Relationships of Itineracy and Salary," *Methodist History,* vol. 21 (October 1982):54-55, claims a similar disparity existed in 1912, when the top one and a half percent of the pastors received three and a half times more salary.

24. See C. Eric Lincoln, *The Black Church in the African American Experience*

(Durham, N.C.: Duke University Press, 1990) and compensation statistics of the Rio Grande and Oklahoma Indian Missionary Conferences.

25. Nolan B. Harmon citing the case of Bishop Costen J. Harrell in "Going to Goshen," *Ministry and Mission,* ed. Barbara Brown Taylor (Atlanta: Post Horn Press, 1985), pp. 161-62.

26. Nolan B. Harmon, *Understanding The United Methodist Church* (Nashville: Abingdon Press, 1977 revised edition), p. 120.

27. Samuel E. Karff, *A Biblical Basis For Ministry,* ed. Earl E. Shelp and Ronald H. Sunderland (Philadelphia: Westminster Press, 1983), p. 13.

28. Prentice M. Gordon, Sr., "Experiencing Covenant Ministry in the United Methodist Connectional and Itinerant System," Doctor of Ministry Project, Emory University, 1983, p. 48.

29. Quoted in "The Ministerial Covenant in The United Methodist Church Today," *Quarterly Review* (Spring 1990):30.

30. Quoted in ibid., pp. 32 and 34.

31. Horace G. Smith in Anderson, *Methodism,* p. 73.

32. Cited from the *National Christian Reporter* of January 12, 1990 in *The Christian Ministry* (May-June 1990):5.

33. See Charles E. Fiquett, Jr., "Does the Itineracy Subsidize Mediocrity," *Circuit Rider* (February 1985):11.

34. Personal correspondence from W. Robb Kell, August 25, 1990.

35. Harmon, *Understanding The United Methodist Church,* p. 124.

36. Norwood, "The Americanization of The Wesleyan Itinerant," p. 62. John Wesley quoted from John Wesley, *The Letters of the Reverend John Wesley,* 8 volumes (London: 1931) A.M., VI, 3, December 1, 1972.

A BIBLIOGRAPHY ON ITINERACY

Archibald, James P. "Our System Still Works." *Circuit Rider,* February 1985.

Armstrong, James, Sally B. Geis, and Donald E. Messer. "Revisioning Itineracy in The United Methodist Church." Unpublished manuscript (Denver: Iliff Institute for Lay and Clergy Education, 1989).

Bayes, Marjorie. "The Effects of Relocation on the Trailing Spouse." Unpublished manuscript.

Brown, Donald G. *The Methodist Appointive System: A Brief History and Case Study.* Emory University, S.T.D., 1970.

Carroll, Jackson, Barbara J. Hargrove, and Adair Lummis. *Women of the Cloth.* New York: Harper and Row, 1983.

Clements, Rosa B. "The Development of a Profile of United Methodist Black Clergywomen in the East Ohio Annual Conference." United Theological Seminary, D.Min. project, 1990.

"Clergy Families in the United Methodist Ministry." Committee on Higher Education and Ministry. *Daily Christian Advocate* Advance Edition. Nashville, Tennessee: General Conference of The United Methodist Church. vol. VI, I-53–I-56.

Coger, Marian. *Women in Parish Ministry: Stress and Support.* Washington, D.C.: Alban Institute, 1985.

Crook, James R. Jr. "Building Understanding Between the Pastor-Parish Relations Committee and the District Superintendent Concerning Consultation in Appointments in The United Methodist Church" Drew University, D.Min. 1987.

Deming, Laura, ed. *Spice,* a monthly publication which is a support system for women and men whose spouses are clergy. Crystal Falls, Michigan: Clergy Family Publications.

Deming, Laura and Jack Stubbs. *Men Married to Ministers.* Alban Institute, 1986.

Denison, Richard E. Jr. A Charge to Keep: Recovering the Itineracy in The United Methodist Church. The University of Chicago, D.Min. 1985.

Duecker, R. Sheldon. *Tensions in the Connection.* Nashville: Abingdon Press, 1983.

Dunlap, E. Dale. "The United Methodist System of Itinerant Ministry." *Rethinking Methodist History,* eds. Russell E. Richey and Kenneth E. Rowe. Nashville: Kingswood Books, 1985.

———. "The United Methodist System of Itinerant Ministry: Its Nature and Future." Occasional Papers No. 30. The United Methodist Board of Higher Education and Ministry, 1980.

———. "The System of Itineracy in American Methodism: An Historical Essay." Unpublished manuscript.

Forbes, Bruce David. "Methodist Mission Among the Dakotas: A Case Study of Difficulties," In *Rethinking Methodist History,* eds. Russell E. Richey and Kenneth E. Rowe. Nashville: Kingswood Books, 1985.

Garrell, Donald K. " 'Ride a Circuit or Let It Alone': Early Practices That Kept The United Brethren, Albright People and Methodists Apart." *Methodist History,* October 1986.

Giffort, Carolyn DeSwarte, ed. *The Nineteenth-Century American Methodist Itinerant Preacher's Wife.* New York: Garland Publishing, 1987.

Gilbert, Barbara G. *Who Ministers to Ministers? A Study of Support Systems for Clergy and Spouses.* Washington, D.C.: The Alban Institute, Inc., 1987.

Gordon, Prentiss M., Sr. "Experiencing Covenant in the United Methodist Connectional Itinerant Ministry." Emory University, D.Min., 1983.

Hall, Russell Charles. "A Study of the United Methodist Itineracy System of Placing Its Pastors in the Central New York Conference." Drew University, D.Min., 1979.

Hancock, Oros L., Jr. "Clergy Needs Which Merit Consideration in the Appointment of United Methodist Ministers in the Western North Carolina Annual Conference." Drew University, D.Min. Project, 1987.

Handy, Robert. "American Methodism and Its Historical Frontier." *Methodist History,* 23:1, October 1984.

Harmon, Nolan B. *Understanding The United Methodist Church.* Nashville: Abingdon Press, 1961.

Hels, Sharon J., ed. "The Ministerial Covenant in The United Methodist Church Today." *Quarterly Review,* Spring 1990.

Hensy, James A. *The Itineracy: Its Power and Peril.* New York: The Methodist Book Concern, 1918.

Holter, Don W. "Some Changes Related to the Ordained Ministry in the History of American Methodism." *Methodist History A.M.E. Zion,* vol. 13, April 1975.

Houk, Ronald A. "Let There Be Justice! But Whose Justice?" *Circuit Rider,* October 1988.

Jeffrey, Julie Roy. "Ministry Through Marriage" in *Women in New Worlds* eds. H. F. Thomas and R. S. Keller. Nashville: Abingdon Press, 1981.

Job, Rueben P. "Christian Ministry in the Third Millennium." Unpublished manuscript, January 8, 1989.

Kim, Illsoo. "Organizational Patterns of Korean-American Methodist Churches: Denominationalism and Personal Community." *Rethinking Methodist History,* eds. Russell E. Richey and Kenneth E. Rowe. Nashville: Kingswood Books, 1985.

Lee, Joon-Young. *New Church Development Strategy: A Case of Collegial Ministry of a Clergy Couple (Korean-American).* School of Theology at Claremont, D.Min., 1987.

London, Harlan. *Clergy Families and Career Paths in the United Methodist Ministry.* Nashville: Division of Ordained Ministry, Board of Higher Education and Ministry, 1983.

Mace, David, and Vera Mace. *What's Happening to Clergy Marriages.* Nashville: Abingdon Press, 1980.

Mathews, James K. *Set Apart to Serve: The Meaning and Role of Episcopacy in the Wesleyan Tradition.* Nashville: Abingdon Press, 1985.

McCollum, Audrey T. *The Trauma of Moving,* vol. 182. Newbury Park, California: Sage Library of Social Research, 1990.

Menking, Stanley J., "The Itineracy Matures." *Circuit Rider,* February 1985.

Messer, Donald E. *Contemporary Images of Christian Ministry.* Nashville: Abingdon Press, 1988.

Mickey, Paul, and Ginny W. Ashmore. *The Clergy Family: Is Normal Life Possible.* Zondervan, 1991.

Miller, Duane R. "Clergy Couples Bring a Time for Change in Our Itineracy." *Circuit Rider,* October 1988.

Mura, Susan Swan. "The Clergy Supply and Demand: Will Too Many Become Too Few?" *Circuit Rider,* July-August 1989.

Neely, Thomas B. *The Minister in the Appointive System.* New York: Fleming H. Revell Company, 1914.

Nickerson, Michael G. "Historical Relationships of Itineracy and Salary," *Methodist History,* vol. 21, October 1982.

Niswander, Bonnie. "Clergy Wives of the New Generation." *Pastoral Psychology,* vol. 30, 1982.

Nordstrom, Carol Shimmin. *Clergy Couples in a Shared Call: A Needed Ministry.* Luther Northwestern Theological Seminary, D.Min., 1987.

Norwood, Frederick A. "The Americanization of the Wesleyan Itinerant." *The Ministry in the Methodist Heritage.* Gerald O. McCulloh, editor. Nashville: The Board of Education of The Methodist Church, 1960, pp. 32-39.

———. "The Church Takes Shape, 1784–1824." *The History of American Methodism,* vol. I, Emory Stevens Bucke, ed. New York: Abingdon Press, 1964.

———. *The Story of American Methodism.* Nashville: Abingdon Press, 1974.

———. *Sourcebook of American Methodism.* Nashville: Abingdon Press, 1982.

Oden, Marilyn Brown. "Stress and Purpose: Clergy Spouses Today." *The Christian Century,* April 20, 1988.

Peck, J. Richard, "Two Hundred Years of Wear." *Circuit Rider,* February 1985.

Proctor-Smith, George L. "Is There (Married) Life After Itineracy? *Circuit Rider,* November/December 1986.

Rediger, G. Lloyd. "Revolution in the Parsonage." *The Christian Ministry,* January 1986.

Rhodes, Lynn N. *Co-Creating: A Feminist Vision of Ministry.* Philadelphia: The Westminster Press, 1987.

Richey, Russell E. "Evolving Patterns of Methodist Ministry." *Methodist History,* vol. 22, October 1983.

Rowe, Kenneth E. "Counting the Converts: Progress Reports as Church History." *Rethinking Methodist History,* eds. Russell E. Richey and Kenneth E. Rowe. Nashville: Kingswood Books, 1985.

Sadio, Sydney Silvester. *Open Itineracy in The United Methodist Church.* Princeton Theological Seminary, 1984.

Schaller, Lyle E. "Is the Problem Clergy Shortage Vs. 'Surplus' Or Is It a Matter of the Optimum Use of Personnel?" *Circuit Rider,* July-August, 1989.

———. "What Will the 1990's Bring?" *The Parish Paper.* vol. 19, no. 7 (Naperville, Ill., January 1990).

Schreckengost, George Earl. *The Effect of Latent Racial, Ethnic, and Sexual Biases on Open Itineracy in East Ohio Conference, The United Methodist Church.* Lancaster Theological Seminary, D.Min. 1984.

Sellers, J. W. *Methodism's Ministry to the Clergy Family Through Its Housing Policies of the Past, Present, and Future.* Drew University, D.Min. 1987.

Sinclair, Donna. *The Pastor's Wife Today.* Nashville: Abingdon Press, 1981.

Smith, Horace Greeley. "The Itinerant Ministry." *Methodism,* ed. William K. Anderson. Cincinnati: The Methodist Publishing House, 1947.

Sweet, Leonard I. *The Minister's Wife: Her Role in Nineteenth-Century American Evangelicalism.* Philadelphia: Temple University Press, 1983.

Thomas, James S. "How Theology Emerges from Polity." *Wesleyan Theology Today.* Ed. Theodore Runyon. Nashville: Kingswood Books, 1985.

Tuell, Jack M. *The Organization of The United Methodist Church.* Revised Edition. Nashville: Abingdon Press, 1985.

Willimon, William H., and Robert L. Wilson, *Rekindling the Flame: Strategies for a Vital United Methodism.* Nashville: Abingdon Press, 1987.

Wimberly, Anne Streaty, and Edward Powell Wimberly. *One Household, One Hope: Building Ethnic Minority Clergy Family Support Networks.* Nashville: Board of Ordained Ministry, 1988.

INDEX